The Energy of Forgiveness

The Energy of Forgiveness

LESSONS FROM THOSE IN RESTORATIVE DIALOGUE

Dr. Mark Umbreit
WITH
Jennifer Blevins
AND
Ted Lewis

FOREWORD BY
Mary Jo Kreitzer

CASCADE *Books* • Eugene, Oregon

THE ENERGY OF FORGIVENESS
Lessons from Those in Restorative Dialogue

Copyright © 2015 Mark Umbreit. All rights reserved. Except for brief quotations in critical publications or reviews, no part of this book may be reproduced in any manner without prior written permission from the publisher. Write: Permissions. Wipf and Stock Publishers, 199 W. 8th Ave., Suite 3, Eugene, OR 97401.

Cascade Publications
An Imprint of Wipf and Stock Publishers
199 W. 8th Ave., Suite 3
Eugene, OR 97401

www.wipfandstock.com

ISBN 13: 978-1-62564-423-7

Cataloguing-in-Publication Data

Umbreit, Mark, 1949–

The energy of forgiveness : lessons from those in restorative dialogue / Mark Umbreit, with Jennifer Blevins and Ted Lewis.

xviii + 120 p. ; 23 cm. Includes bibliographical references.

ISBN 13: 978-1-62564-423-7

1. Conflict management. 2. Restorative Justice. 3. Victims of crimes. I. Umbreit, Mark. II. Blevins, Jennifer. III. Lewis, Ted. IV. Title.

HM1126 .U35 2015

Manufactured in the U.S.A.   07/29/2015

Authentic Forgiveness

Authentic forgiveness is a gift of awakening, a freeing of one's spirit, a release of long-held, toxic energy. Forgiveness is more of a direction than a destination, a way of life grounded in an attitude of humility and compassion. Authentic forgiveness has little to do with moral obligations or externally imposed values.

—Mark Umbreit, 2009

Contents

Illustrations | ix
Foreword by Mary Jo Kreitzer | xi
Preface by Mark Umbreit | xiii
Contributors | xvii

CHAPTER 1   The Energy of Forgiveness: A Gift of Awakening | 1
CHAPTER 2   Restorative Dialogue: A Path to Healing the Wounds | 13

Forgiveness for Victims of Crime

CHAPTER 3   A Burglary Leads to a Lasagna Meal | 25
CHAPTER 4   A Tragic Car Crash Gives Way to Reconciliation | 31
CHAPTER 5   A Mother Goes to Prison to Get Some Answers | 34
CHAPTER 6   A Woman Connects with Her Father's Murderer | 38

Forgiveness for Families

CHAPTER 7   A Broken Family Comes Together | 47
CHAPTER 8   A Daughter Journeys from Incest to Healing | 51

Forgiveness in Schools

CHAPTER 9   A Circle of Sixty Overcomes Racism | 59
CHAPTER 10   A Classroom Out of Control Opens Up | 63

Contents

Forgiveness in Workplaces

CHAPTER 11   A Hospital Staff Transcends Workplace Tensions | 69
CHAPTER 12   A Nonprofit Agency Finds a New Beginning | 73

Forgiveness for Communities

CHAPTER 13   An Act of Vandalism Engages a High School | 79
CHAPTER 14   A Neo-Nazi Youth Offers to Apologize | 83
CHAPTER 15   A 9/11 Death Threat Opens a Door for Muslims | 87
CHAPTER 16   A Community Circle Changes Everyone's Hearts | 92
CHAPTER 17   An Offender Takes Part in His Victim's Family | 97

Closing Thoughts

CHAPTER 18   Bearing Witness to Strength and Resilience | 101

Appendices

APPENDIX 1   The Language of Energy for Conflict and Resolution: More than a Metaphor | 107
APPENDIX 2   Fostering the Energy of Forgiveness Within Ourselves and Others: Practices to Foster the Energy of Forgiveness | 118
APPENDIX 3   Mindfulness, Deep Listening, and Stories: The Spiritual Core of Peacemaking | 124

Bibliography | 129

Illustrations

FIGURE 1   Steps for Centering | 7
FIGURE 2   Circle Process Guidelines | 16
FIGURE 3   Circle Process | 17

Foreword

IN *THE ENERGY OF Forgiveness*, Mark Umbreit with Jennifer Blevins and Ted Lewis describes in exquisite detail many paths for achieving wholeness and healing through forgiveness. The underlying premise of the book is that if we connect with the suffering of others, tame our egos and embrace humility, cultivate mindfulness and presence, and tap into the healing power of story, we can move beyond human conflict and achieve reconciliation. Up front, they acknowledge that this journey is not for the timid and is one that requires deep courage.

The book details practices that prepare one for facing deep conflict and trauma such as being mindful in the present moment and nonjudgmental; using the practice of *centering* so that we can quiet our minds and be present; being authentic and not hiding behind a façade; and deeply listening with compassion and the intent to understand. These practices ultimately prepare one to both listen to and tell a story within a context in which there has been intense conflict and trauma. As the authors note, the power of story has been used throughout the ages and in many indigenous traditions to achieve healing.

Using the power of story, the core of the book is wrapped around real-life stories of people who participated in restorative dialogue and engaged the energy of forgiveness. The stories are riveting and tap into many life situations including crime and violence, and trauma within families, schools, the workplace, and communities.

As I reflect on the contribution that this book makes, two things stand out. One is that healing and wholeness are attainable even in situations where inconceivable pain and injustice has been experienced. And second, preparation and skillful facilitation can make all the difference. In story after story, I found myself reflecting on how important creating a safe space was in giving people the tools to be present and prepared for what

Foreword

emerged. This book will be very valuable to people who have experienced loss, trauma, and violence, and to those who support them.

Mary Jo Kreitzer PhD, RN, FAAN
Founder and Director, Center for Spirituality and Healing,
University of Minnesota

Preface

THE POWER OF FORGIVENESS to heal wounds and foster growth is widely recognized in nearly all faith traditions, many secular practices, and in the literature of psychology. Over the past decades volumes of articles, books, and films have addressed the power, value, and importance of forgiveness. Many of these have come from various religious traditions. Many more have developed independent of any connection to a religion or even a higher power in a more general sense. All have offered numerous examples of forgiveness, often times in the most unlikely context, along with a plan to practice forgiveness in one's life and community. Authors have frequently advocated a logical, linear, step-by-step process of precisely how to forgive.

All of these articles, books, and films provide helpful insight into understanding the concept of forgiveness. And yet most fail to embrace the mystery of forgiveness, the paradox of forgiveness, the energetic language of forgiveness that goes far beneath the words and intellectual or theological concepts. And few even address the enhanced power of engaging the energy of forgiveness when doing so in the presence of the person who harmed them, particularly through a form of restorative dialogue.

Nowhere in the extensive literature on forgiveness will you find recognition of the highly toxic nature of even the word *forgiveness* in many communities or among many individuals. People directly involved in the intense, historical, and violent political conflicts found in so many countries, including the United States, as well as individual survivors of violent criminal conflict, have often made this clear. For many, to even mention the word *forgiveness* is to diminish the harm caused, to deny the legitimate intense anger felt by the survivor. There are few other areas of human communication that bring us so deep into the territory of unintended negative consequences. Our well-intended comments can trigger people, shut them down, and even re-traumatize them in some cases. So restorative justice and dialogue is not about pushing forgiveness upon others. It is about

Preface

creating a safe place and process where people choose to engage the energy of forgiveness if that is what they need, with no inducement or direction by the facilitator. Forgiveness is profoundly an inner experience, but at the same time it always involves a relational dynamic, and thus dialogue sets a new and powerful thing in motion: an unburdening for both parties.

And here lies the paradox of forgiveness, the mystery to which we stand in awe. The less said directly about forgiveness in the preparation and facilitation of a restorative dialogue the more likely many people choose to go there, entirely of their own volition. The deepest expressions of forgiveness often occur when the word is never mentioned, when the people involved might even choke on the word. Yet the energy of forgiveness is communicated through the most impactful form of human communication, the language of our bodies, the nonverbal language of our hearts, and through this all are led to a major shift in the tone and tenor of relationships, to a greater sense of release, peace, and transformation. Rather than focusing on the language of forgiveness, some people discover that forgiveness has happened after they feel something being lifted from them (which both parties can experience).

Through my work over the past four decades in restorative justice dialogue among victims of severe violence, including family members of homicide victims, and among communities in entrenched, violent conflict, including those in Northern Ireland, Africa, and the Middle East, I have been fortunate to bear witness to such energetic expressions of forgiveness. At times the word *forgiveness* might emerge in the facilitated restorative dialogue, but certainly with different meanings attached to it. In most cases, the word *forgiveness* is never expressed, particularly in long-standing, violent, political conflict. In all of these cases the shift in energy, attitude, empathy, and communication among the involved parties is palpable.

Special thanks is due to the Fetzer Institute which provided generous support for the research that led to this book and the drafting of the manuscript. Completion of this book would not have been possible without the tremendous editorial assistance of Jennifer Blevins and Ted Lewis, both valued colleagues at the Center for Restorative Justice and Peacemaking at the University of Minnesota, where I serve as the founding director.

This book bears witness to powerful and real-life stories of the energy of forgiveness in families, schools, communities, workplaces, and in response to crime and violence. Each case has its own unique characteristics. All share many common threads that we weave together in an attempt to more clearly understand and honor this mystery that goes beneath words and cognitive awareness. Our broader understanding of what we mean by the "energy of forgiveness" as well as practices that can foster the energy of forgiveness within our lives are offered at the end of the book. May you find peace and strength in the journey of engaging the power and mystery of the energy of forgiveness.

Mark Umbreit, PhD

Contributors

Mark Umbreit, PhD, Professor of Social Work at the University of Minnesota, and Founder/Director of the Center for Restorative Justice and Peacemaking.

Jennifer Blevins, MSW, Community Faculty of Social Work at the University of Minnesota, PhD candidate, and Research Assistant for the Center for Restorative Justice and Peacemaking.

Ted Lewis, MA, Director of Communications for the Center for Restorative Justice and Peacemaking at the University of Minnesota, restorative justice trainer, mediator, and consultant.

CHAPTER 1

The Energy of Forgiveness: A Gift of Awakening

FORGIVENESS IS A VERY toxic word for many people. It suggests a denial of tremendous harm, disrespect, and trauma that has occurred. To even suggest forgiving the perpetrator or person responsible for causing harm, for many but not all, seems inconceivable.

There are also many people who in their minds would never forgive the person or groups who harmed them, yet who appear to have achieved a level of peace within their life, no longer consumed by hatred. These individuals often experience similar physiological and emotional benefits that researchers have found can result from explicit acts of forgiveness. People who are more forgiving report fewer health problems. A study by Dr. Fred Luskin found that forgiveness leads to less stress and fewer physical symptoms of stress, as well as reduced anger and reduced depression.[1] Luskin found that the failure to forgive may be more important than hostility as a risk factor for heart disease. A higher incidence of illnesses such as cardiovascular disease and cancer were found among those individuals who blame other people for their troubles. Furthermore, Luskin found that those who imagine not forgiving someone showed negative changes in blood pressure, muscle tension, and immune response. Similar outcomes have been found by a growing number of researchers who have examined the impact of thoughtful, verbal expressions of forgiveness. Even people with the most devastating losses can learn to forgive and feel better psychologically and emotionally.[2]

---

1. Luskin, *Forgive for Good*, 86–87.
2. Ibid., 99–101.

So how can those who never spoke the words of forgiveness or even those who experience the entire notion of forgiveness as very toxic exhibit similar characteristics to what this research on forgiveness has found? Are cases where people deny having forgiven but have found peace in their situation truly "forgiveness"? Is expressing the words "I forgive you" always necessary? Does it matter, if one's life becomes less stressful and more at peace as a result of seeing the humanity and woundedness in the person who caused harm? Is there a process for allowing this disempowering of hatred to occur? Does this require an intellectual understanding of what is happening? Or, is it about accepting the unexplainable yet beautiful mystery of life? Such is the focus of this book. Not to intellectualize, analyze, and develop a theory of what is actually happening in the process of healing from past harm, but to bear witness to the remarkable resilience, compassion, and kindness of the human spirit.

All of the multitude of books, research, and films on forgiveness provide important and necessary information, yet these resources are not sufficient in beginning to understand and witness the mysterious and remarkable energy of forgiveness. This requires us to go beneath the words and theories of forgiveness; the intellectual and theological constructs. It requires us to look deeper within ourselves, to find the courage to embark on a spiritual (not necessarily religious) journey, to connect with the suffering of all people, to humble ourselves and tame our egos, to be mindful and authentic in our presence with others, and ultimately to honor the healing power of story and the precious gift of life we have all been given.

We Are Spiritual Beings on a Human Journey

Religion and spirituality are often considered to be one and the same, both closely aligned with the concept of forgiveness. While the two can overlap, they can be quite distinct from each other. Rachel Naomi Remen, a gifted physician, author, and teacher who works with end-stage cancer patients and health professionals, has a beautiful way a clarifying this distinction.[3] Religion is by definition a set of beliefs and dogma, a way of explaining the deeper meaning of life and the relationship to a higher power. Religions tend to be mutually exclusive and highly judgmental, with each claiming their own version of the truth about human existence and higher power.

---

3. Remen, "Spirit: Resource for Healing," 66.

The Energy of Forgiveness: A Gift of Awakening

For many, religion can be the starting point and a helpful bridge to a deeper experience of spirituality. Getting stuck in the dogma and rituals, however, can often become an obstacle to crossing over to deeper experience of spirituality. For others, religion itself has become the obstacle because of the perceived hypocrisy and woundedness they have experienced. These individuals have no bridge. They seek their own pathways to spirituality and healing outside of organized religions. Spirituality is profoundly nonexclusive. It embraces the core wisdom—not the dogma and politics—of all of the world's religions and recognizes the interconnectedness of all beings.

Spirituality is inseparable from a lifelong quest for authentic meaning in life, relationship to a higher power, and openness to the incredible mystery of life. For those seeking a deeper experience of forgiveness and/or spirituality, the journey is anchored in a spirit of humility and compassion for all, not arrogance, rigid belief of one's truth, and behavior that is harmful to others. Ultimately, in spite of our often fragmented world, a search for wholeness inspires us to look deeper and move beyond human conflict to reconcile all of who we are.

The Search for Wholeness

Ever-increasing busyness and multitasking characterizes most of our lives, often keeping us from what we truly cherish. Our warp-speed culture leads to a disconnected way of being. The power of the mind and ego dominates our behavior, with the belief that we can master and control events in our lives. The needs of our physical bodies as well as our souls are frequently ignored. Stress, a leading cause of health problems, not only leads to conflict and less helpful ways of responding to traumatic events, it also leads to frequent "burnout" in jobs and even relationships.

The search for wholeness in our lives is about integrating and nurturing all dimensions of our being; the mind, body, and spirit. It is about seeking a more balanced way of living, where the power of the mind is tamed and the needs of our body and the yearnings of our soul and spirit are uplifted. It manifests in such disparate forms as exercise, stretching, healthy diet, walks outside, good sleep, meditation or prayer, studying inspirational books, literature, film or the arts, or even baseball.

Wholeness is also about accessing the wisdom of the heart, about balance and learning. In the words of Louis Farmer, an Onondaga American Indian Elder, "A good heart and a good mind—these are what you need to be a chief."[4] A continually active mind that is not balanced by the heart can become a tyrant. A compassionate heart that is not balanced by the mind can be ineffective in responding to conflicts and traumatic events. This balance can be better understood as we explore energy as the life force that connects everything living and impacts all of our interactions, whether perceived as good or bad.

Honor the Energy of Life

Within Western culture, the concept of energy is that of a commodity to be sold and purchased. The word *energy* is widely used in terms of fueling our cars, heating our homes, powering our many appliances, supporting computer technology and the Internet, or providing the means for supporting our body's ability to perform various tasks. It would be hard to avoid hearing or seeing the term *energy* as a commodity for purchase in our daily lives. Yet, when energy is spoken of as the life force, the core essence of our humanness, the vibrational interconnectedness of all beings, and the language of our souls, many in Western cultures become uneasy, skeptical, or highly judgmental about such "irrelevant new age psychobabble." Indigenous cultures throughout the world, including the more than 500 well-developed tribal communities that inhabited America before any European ever stepped on the continent, have for centuries recognized and honored the unseen mysterious powers of the universe, the spiritual nature of all beings, the interconnectedness of all beings and things, and the wisdom of nature and the animal world. Though they didn't use the term *energy*, these beliefs speak to the authentic language and wisdom of the soul, our energetic presence among others and in the world. Shamans and mystics from many ancient cultures have spoken of the oneness and interconnectedness of human existence.

Quantum physicists speak of this same reality as matter and energy being two poles of the same unity. One of the most well-known and brilliant scientists of the past century, Albert Einstein, challenged the basic assumptions about the universe with his theory of relativity. He opened the doors of science to even consider mystical realities. Einstein theorized that space and time are intertwined and that matter is inseparable from an ever-present quantum energy that represents the sole reality behind all appearances. Bell's Theorem, a quantum physics law, says than once connected,

---

4. Quoted in Schaef, *Native Wisdom for White Minds* (no page number).

The Energy of Forgiveness: A Gift of Awakening

objects affect one another forever no matter where they are, suggesting that an invisible stream of energy will always connect any two objects that have been connected in any way in the past.[5] For a small but growing number of scientists a deeper understanding of physics has led them to explore metaphysics, the unseen mystery of life, the fundamental nature of reality and meaning. Metaphysics is often perceived as the knowledge-based dimension of spirituality.

The energy behind all of our communications, verbal and nonverbal, influences the manner in which we respond to severe conflicts or traumatic events, as well as how we are perceived by those who have caused harm. It is central to facing the issue, allowing toxic energy to be released in healthy ways, and finding peace as we experience transformation and healing, perhaps even forgiveness.

The martial art of aikido can help us embrace conflict as a prime motivator for change in our lives, viewing conflict as an opportunity for nurturing growth in ourselves and in our relationships.[6] Aikido is a highly sophisticated Japanese martial art designed to resolve physical conflict by making an attack harmless without doing harm to the attacker. The literal translation of aikido means "the way of blending energies." Aikido offers a useful metaphor for shifting our way of thinking and responding to conflict, from domination or problem solving to the blending of energies to co-create a more satisfying, collaborative, or even transformative resolution of the conflict. Thomas Crum calls this the *aiki* approach, working with the energy of conflict, which for some can lead to experiencing the energy of forgiveness.[7]

When strong emotions of anger and judgment are directed at us by people with whom we are in conflict, the normal response is to become defensive and to fight back, verbally challenging and attacking the other person. Using the wisdom of aikido and awareness of the energy that drives conflict, we can render the verbal attack harmless without harming the other person, by allowing the toxic energy of the other to be released. It is possible to deflect those verbal attacks without letting them hook our ego, and to respond to the other person with a very different, more calm and respectful energy, which is disarming in its own way. Our energy can communicate the message that we do not plan to fight back. This may sound

---

5. Shimony, "Bells' Theorem."
6. Crum, *The Magic of Conflict*, 40–42.
7. Ibid., 83.

good in theory, yet the wisdom of an "*aiki* approach" is not found in verbal expression alone or intellectual knowledge about aikido. It requires being emotionally, physically, and spiritually centered, what Buddhists would refer to as taming the mind, or the ego.

Becoming centered is achieved through deep breathing and mindfulness of our own energy. If we are not able to center ourselves in the midst of stress or anger, the aikido approach is not likely to be effective in traveling the path of openness to the energy of forgiveness and healing. When our egos are hooked in the midst of conflict, the energy felt by others, regardless of the well-intended words we speak, is likely to escalate the conflict. In fact we can say the exact same words—such as, "Why do you feel that way about me?" or "Did you ever think about how this is affecting others?" or "I feel hurt and misunderstood"—and they can be heard with entirely different meanings based on the energy of our presence, our tone of voice, our posture, our comfort with moments of silence, or our ability to listen deeply to the other without judgment. Being centered and mindful, embraced as a way of life, can significantly change the tone, experience, and impact of our communication with others.

Mindfulness as a Way of Life

Engaging the energy of forgiveness can be greatly facilitated by practicing mindfulness as a way of life, trying to be in a constant state of "open hearted moment by moment non-judgmental awareness."[8] Mindfulness is a very specific process and practice to affect perceptions and behaviors. Coming from Buddhist wisdom, the practice of mindfulness is now offered in thousands of communities throughout the Western world. Over the years, Dr. Jon Kabat-Zinn, founder and Director of the Stress Reduction Clinic and the Center for Mindfulness, Health Care, and Society at the University of Massachusetts Medical School, has taught mindfulness-based stress reduction to thousands of individuals. He has been a pioneer in bridging the gap between doctors and other health care professionals in championing the power of mindfulness.

Like spirituality, mindfulness is a way of being, a way of life. It is far more than just a practice of meditation, yoga, or similar activity. Mindfulness is about embracing a nonjudgmental attitude toward people and events in a way that does not drain our energy and emotions. It can lead

---

8. Kabat-Zinn, *Coming to Our Senses*, 108.

The Energy of Forgiveness: A Gift of Awakening

to greater understanding of self and others, and a greater ability to detach ourselves from behaviors and perceptions in which we get stuck. Mindfulness allows us to accept the present-moment reality and to be fully present with others, in a more humble, focused, and compassionate manner. While people may engage in many different healthy activities on their path to mindful living, centering of our mind and spirit is a daily core practice from cultures around the world that provides a starting place for mindfulness as a way of life.

Centering our Mind and Spirit

Centering is a process of quieting our minds, taming our egos, and becoming very focused on the present moment through an increased sense of peace and awareness. It is finding the still point of power within ourselves, not power to control or manipulate, but power to be fully present in an authentic manner that integrates the strength of body, mind, and spirit. When we are centered we are far less likely to get hooked into conflict or thrown off balance by various events in our lives. Centering is the gateway to deeper practices of meditation and healing. Centering is also an incredibly practical technique used by Olympic athletes, martial artists, professional dancers, and other athletes and artists committed to performing at their best. It is essential to engaging the spirit and energy of forgiveness in our lives.

Centering one's self is the first step of a humanistic approach to respond to severe conflict and traumatic events. It is a very helpful way of adjusting our energy and consciousness to the needs of the present moment.

> **A basic and easy form of centering follows these steps:**
> 1. Sit comfortably in a chair, with your back and neck erect.
> 2. Begin practicing deep, slow belly breathing, counting to eight as you inhale and counting to eight as you exhale.
> 3. Pay attention to your breath as it enters and leaves your nostrils, or to the rising and falling of your abdomen as you breathe in and out.
> 4. Imagine a beautiful place in nature that brings you peace.
> 5. If your mind wanders and you are having a hard time concentrating, which is very likely to occur, focus again on your breath, slow and deep belly breathing to the count of eight.
> 6. Continue for three to five minutes, twice a day, or whenever you are facing particularly stressful situations.

The Gift of Authentic Presence

To be fully present and authentic with another is one of life's greatest gifts. We certainly are with many different people each day of our lives. Yet our common interactions with others tend to be task-oriented, functional, brief, and superficial. How often does even a good friend respond in an honest and real manner to the frequent question, "How are you doing?"

Virginia Satir, the late internationally recognized family therapist, spoke of the healing power of being fully present with others as a central element of her life's work.[9] Satir was deeply grounded in a humanistic approach to working with people, believing in each person's capacity for growth, change, and transformation. She viewed authentic human connection as fundamental to change processes in the lives of those struggling with conflicted feelings and events. Satir had a powerful presence with others, because she remained connected to her belief system of authenticity at her core being.

Drawing upon the influence of Satir, family therapist and mediator Lois Gold identified four elements of presence that can increase our effectiveness in being of service to others: (1) Being centered; (2) Being connected to one's governing values, beliefs, and highest purpose; (3) Connecting with the humanity of the other person; and (4) Being congruent, a condition of being emotionally honest, that is being in touch with who you are, and not allowing your anxiety, pride, or ego to be a mask.[10] When we are authentically present with others, we are capable of listening deeply and compassionately, making it possible to connect with the suffering and humanity of even those with whom serious conflict or trauma has occurred.

Deep Compassionate Listening

Many of us have been trained in active listening, a process of giving periodic verbal feedback to the other person to indicate that you are "hearing them" and are validating their concerns. This technique often involves periodically summarizing their comments through a verbal statement of "I understand that your primary concerns are . . . ," or asking for clarification through a statement of "Am I right in understanding that . . . ?" or "Could you tell me more about that? I'm a bit confused." In difficult negotiations or

---

9. Satir, "The Therapist Story," 23.
10. Gold, "Influencing Unconscious Influences," 252–53.

even everyday conversations with friends or family members about specific plans for an activity or project, there is no better way to check our assumptions and make sure everyone is on the same page than through active listening. As good as active listening can be, it can also become a major blockage to allowing the healing energy of story to flow as is necessary. Active listening, by definition, keeps us in our head. It must, so that we can accurately paraphrase or summarize comments.

Deep compassionate listening is quite different and requires another approach. It requires us to listen to each other in our wholeness, the language of our body and spirit as well as the language of the mind. Deep compassionate listening requires us to listen from the heart, to quiet our mind and ego, and to allow the healing energy of story to emerge. It requires a conscious effort to avoid fixating solely on understanding the verbal content being expressed, and be open to looking for the emotional energy underneath the language, which may be quite inconsistent with the words being expressed. While learning active listening is relatively easy because of the specific techniques involved, learning deep compassionate listening requires a different path. Deep listening is a way of being, rather than a way of doing. It is not about technique and has everything to do with the energy of one's presence, and one's own groundedness in humility and compassion. Deep compassionate listening, from the heart, rather than problem solving from the mind, changes the way people are present with one another in times of conflict or stress.

Saving Face

A concept that is little understood in Western culture, yet can play a powerful role in dealing with conflicts, negotiating agreements, or experiencing the energy of forgiveness, is that of "saving face," a concept grounded in compassion and humility that originated in China. Police, public trials, and prison are humiliating for all involved. Saving face can be a key strength to a restorative approach. The term "face" is related to one's status and respect among friends, colleagues, or within a family. It is based on one's self-perception of prestige, honor, and reputation in a social context, and therefore is something that is emotionally invested with the powerful energy of the ego. Face can be lost, maintained, or enhanced, and must be constantly attended to in interactions. If self-respect or face is threatened, one can rigidly maintain positions that are even against one's own self-interest. Honoring the importance of self-respect, or face, can for many be more important than solving a problem in a mutually beneficial manner.

Eastern cultures are far more aware of the negative energy of losing face that can block the flow of open, creative energy to resolve conflicts. While the concept of face comes from Eastern cultures, the intrinsic wisdom of trying not to shame our adversaries and to provide opportunities for maintaining one's dignity, honor, and reputation applies to all cultures. Giving the other person space to maintain his or her dignity and not feel demeaned or shamed is central to both a humanistic response to conflict and effective negotiation in general. It helps open the door to honor the story of ourselves and others, as a significant step in the process of healing and finding forgiveness in your heart.

Honor the Healing Power of Story

In Western culture, our typical approach to conflict is problem solving. We ask: What are the issues in dispute? Do the parties have clear needs? Can we identify some common ground? How do we fix this? A clear written agreement is required in formal conflict resolution processes. In many efforts at conflict resolution there is little interest or tolerance for hearing the larger story behind the language of the presenting issues of the conflict. Precisely because of the emotional energy in the stories of the involved parties, many mediators are fearful that having disputants reflect upon and share their stories with each other will not be constructive, and therefore should be avoided. Those stories, however, contain the emotional energy that is fueling the conflict. They provide the real-life context, experience, and perspectives of those in the conflict. Without a healthy outlet for the release of that toxic energy, it will continue to provide power to the conflict, despite the existence of written agreements.

Creating a safe place for people experiencing intense conflict to tell their story without interruptions has been found throughout the ages to be at the core of healing. Personal stories of conflict or trauma touch others as no crisp, articulate argument ever could. Arguments and positions keep us in the head. The telling of stories touches our hearts. Daniel Taylor, in his book *The Healing Power of Stories*, speaks of how stories help us learn to live more responsibly, to understand others in their life context, and to avoid many of the conflicts in life that so quickly hook us.[11]

11. Taylor, *The Healing Power of Stories*.

The Energy of Forgiveness: A Gift of Awakening

When people have found the strength within themselves to directly face a severe conflict or traumatic event, often what is needed is simply someone to share the journey, offer periodic feedback and support, and to avoid problem solving or advice giving. We then need to bear witness rather than get lost in problem solving or advice giving. This is not about intervening through counseling or active mediation of a conflict. Bearing witness is about honoring the strength and resilience of people on a healing journey. It's about an awakening that comes from embracing the energy of forgiveness when recognizing and respecting the imperfect humanity of others as well as ourselves.

The Search for Meaning

Being with the energy of forgiveness, as a gift of awakening, is often connected to our yearning for meaning in our lives. The search for meaning is why people pursue growth, and why some will face the source of their conflict or trauma to make sense of the terrible harm they have experienced. The search for meaning in our lives goes far beyond the everyday issues we face. It goes beyond all of the values, explanations, and even dogma that have entered our lives from external sources, such as our parents or other family members, our faith communities, our teachers, or our governments. The search for meaning is grounded in our yearning for a deeper, heartfelt understanding of our purpose in life. In the search for meaning, we wrestle with questions like why bad things happen to so many people, what happens when we die, and why there is so much cruelty to others by the very people who profess such beautiful values of goodwill and taking care of others. The search for meaning is about finding our own path, our own way of understanding the gift of life.

Victor Frankl's classic book *Man's Search for Meaning* speaks of his experience in a Nazi concentration camp during World War II.[12] Even in the midst of such horror, unspeakable suffering, and mass extermination of human beings, it was his will to live, his search for meaning and kindness in its most simple form, and his hope for the future that kept him from giving up and falling into deep despair and disillusionment. Dr. Frankl, as both a concentration camp survivor and a psychologist, concludes that the meaning of life can be found in each moment of living. Life never ceases to have

---

12. Frankl, *Man's Search for Meaning*, 155–63.

meaning, even in severe conflicts, suffering, and death; even as we struggle with intense anger and acts that we believe are unforgiveable.

In the following chapters we will share numerous real-life stories of people who participated in some form of restorative dialogue and engaged the energy of forgiveness even when the words and intellectual concept of forgiveness were absent. These stories of conflict and trauma come from within families, schools, workplaces, communities, and even in response to crime and violence.

We will first go on to describe what exactly we mean by "restorative dialogue," this common experience in all of the stories that clearly triggered a shift in energy among those present, and allowed former adversaries the opportunity to engage the energy of forgiveness. The book will conclude with specific practices to foster the energy of forgiveness in our lives, some of which you were introduced to in this chapter.

CHAPTER 2

Restorative Dialogue: A Path to Healing the Wounds

RESTORATIVE DIALOGUE IS A process of creating a safe place in which the involved parties can listen deeply to each other's story and perception of a conflict, without attempting to persuade the other, with the goals of humanizing the conflict and repairing the emotional or physical harm to the greatest extent possible. As a mindfulness-based approach to conflict that is grounded in openhearted, moment-by-moment nonjudgmental awareness and deep listening, restorative dialogue attempts to engage the language of the heart as well as the mind.

Working with the energy of our body, mind, and spirit through breath work and centering as described in chapter one is central to restorative dialogue and authentic communication. A spirit of compassion and humility, rather than professional expertise or righteousness, leads to authentic communication and healing. Restorative dialogue is not a quick fix. While problem solving can be important, restorative dialogue is far more concerned about healing and transformation of relationships among those in conflict, with no expectation that all must see "eye to eye" or agree on all issues.

Examples of restorative dialogue that are widely used and empirically grounded through research conducted in North America and other parts of the world include: small group conferencing (often referred to as victim-offender mediation or dialogue); larger group conferencing (often referred to as family and/or community group conferencing); and peacemaking circles (also referred to as talking or healing circles). The circle process is a particularly effective way of dealing with many conflicts or misunderstandings in small or larger groups.

Where Does It Come From?

The contemporary roots of restorative dialogue are found in the restorative justice movement that began in North America in the mid-1970s and today is a global movement widely practiced and endorsed by numerous private and governmental agencies, including the United Nations and the European Union. Restorative justice views crime as a wound within the community and justice requires accountability and healing, not simply costly punishment that frequently results in many unintended negative consequences such as increased criminal sophistication, behavior, and violence, not to mention re-victimization of the victim through the criminal justice system. While restorative justice began in the juvenile and criminal justice systems, today the principles and practices of restorative justice are widely used in many other settings, such as families, schools, workplaces, faith communities, and regional and national contexts.

At a deeper level, many ancient traditions of conflict resolution found in numerous indigenous cultures throughout the world embodied several restorative justice principles. Examples of indigenous justice practices that reflected many restorative values include: peacemaking and talking circles among Native Americans and First Nations People of Canada; the practice of *ho'oponopono* among Native Hawaiians; *palava* huts in Liberia; *Gacaca* village courts in Rwanda; the *sulha* peacemaking process among Arabs and Palestinians; and the *jirga* councils in Afghanistan.

Restorative dialogue builds upon the lengthy experience of many types of dialogue initiatives over past decades. All forms of dialogue are intrinsically good and conducive to healthy conflict resolution. Conventional and widely used approaches to dialogue are highly cognitive, problem-solving oriented, and focused on increased intellectual understanding of the complexity of the presenting issues. While this conventional approach is important and necessary, it is not sufficient. A more contemplative and mindfulness-based approach is a different way of understanding and responding to conflict and trauma. As an approach grounded in an open-hearted, moment-by-moment, nonjudgmental awareness, the focus is on honoring the enormous healing power of story rather than simply obtaining a thorough intellectual understanding of the issue.

What is the Circle Process?

The circle process (often referred to as talking circles, peacemaking circles, or healing circles) establishes a very different style of communication than what most people from European tradition are accustomed. It draws upon the wisdom of the indigenous people of North America and their traditional practices, while not appropriating the full ceremony of the circle process and ritual that is deeply rooted in Native American and Canadian First Nations communities. Rather than aggressive debate and challenging each other, which is common in settings often involving only a few more assertive individuals, the circle process establishes a safe, nonhierarchical space in which all present have the opportunity to speak without interruptions. Rather than active verbal facilitation, communication is regulated through the passing of a talking piece (an object of special meaning or symbolism to the circle facilitator and participants). The talking piece fosters respectful listening and reflection. It prevents one-on-one debating or attacking. After brief opening comments by the circle keeper (facilitator) about the purpose of the talking circle, listing of ground rules and asking for additional contributions to the ground rules, the circle facilitator says a few things about the talking piece and then passes it to the person on the left, clockwise. Only the person with the talking piece can speak. If others jump in with comments, the circle facilitator reminds them of the ground rules and refocuses on the person with the talking piece.

Participants are not required to speak; this would create an unsafe, pressured tone in the circle. If someone feels unable to speak, they can simply pass the talking piece to the next person. The circle process has been brought into European culture by many over the years, including community activists in the restorative justice movement and activists in the feminist movement, most notably Christine Baldwin.[1] Another excellent resource is *The Little Book of Circle Processes,* by Kay Pranis.[2]

Participants in the circle should be invited to share important values that they would want to be honored within the process of communication in the circle. Suggested guidelines for the circle process include: (1) Listen with respect; (2) Each person gets a chance to talk; (3) One person talks at a time; (4) Don't cut people off; (5) Speak for yourself and not as the representative of any group; (6) It's okay to disagree; and (7) No name-calling

---

1. Baldwin, *Calling the Circle.*
2. Pranis, *The Little Book of Circle Process,* 11–18.

or attacking. Suggested guidelines for participation in the circle should be presented in a manner with which those present will feel comfortable. This may mean using different words or examples that are consistent with guidelines, but speak to cultural or group relevance.

> **Circle Process Guidelines and Meaning:**
>
> 1. Listening from the heart
>   - attentive
>   - sincere
>   - bearing witness
>   - not reactive
>   - deep compassionate listening
>
> 2. Speaking from the heart
>   - honesty
>   - from our own true stories
>   - sharing our journey
>   - not philosophical or abstract
>
> 3. Speaking concisely
>   - clarity
>   - simplicity of language
>   - lean speech
>   - not verbose or rambling
>
> 4. Spontaneity
>   - not a prepared statement
>   - not rehearsed
>   - honest

Talking circles are an excellent format to deal with common conflicts we face in our lives. They also serve as a process to facilitate discussion in classes and training seminars to actively engage participants in the sharing of perspectives with respectful, nonjudgmental deep listening. Jack Zimmerman and Virginia Coyle, in *The Way of Council*, offer a solid seven-step framework for conducting the circle process (see diagram).[3]

3. Zimmerman and Coyle, *The Way of Council*.

Restorative Dialogue: A Path to Healing the Wounds

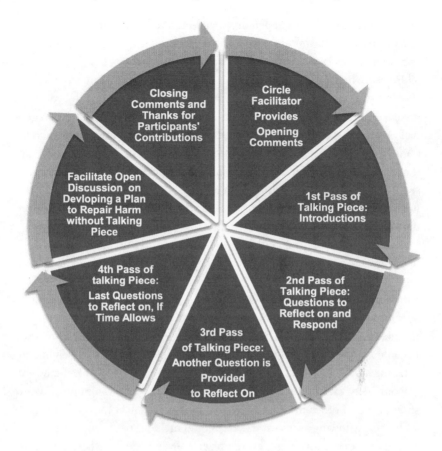

Preparing to Facilitate a Restorative Dialogue Process

The restorative dialogue process begins even before the actual circle meeting by preparing the involved parties before bringing them together face-to-face. This typically involves at least one separate meeting with the parties, and often more meetings, to listen to their concerns, expectations, and needs. These separate preparation meetings are the single most distinguishing characteristic of restorative dialogue, as opposed to other forms of mediation or discussions. The separate meetings help clarify expectations, build rapport between the facilitator and the involved parties, reduce some of the anxiety about the eventual face-to-face meeting with those on the other side of the issue, and clear the path for a safe and authentic encounter with those who are in conflict.

Contact the person or persons invited to the circle who are in conflict and arrange a time and place to meet that is workable within all schedules and where all feel safe. Also briefly discuss any specific needs or issues to be addressed when you come together.

As preparation for the circle moves forward, continually give the involved parties choice in issues that emerge, such as: when the dialogue will occur; where it will be held; preference for an opening ritual such as a moment of silence, prayer, or reading of a verse or poem; if and who the parties would prefer to have as support people to witness the dialogue; seating arrangement in a circle or at a table; and other related issues. This helps build trust and security as people voluntarily choose to embark on the restorative dialogue process together.

Centering and preparation is equally important for someone opting to lead a restorative dialogue circle among family and friends, as it is for a neutral, skilled facilitator. Prepare yourself in mind and body before communicating with the person or persons with whom you are in conflict. Specifically, be mindful of your own energy. Are you tense, rushed, angry, multitasking, impatient, or breathing shallowly? If so, take a few moments to center yourself by breathing in slowly and deep to the count of eight and exhaling slowly to the count of eight. As you breathe in deeply, be aware of your belly expanding and then contracting as you exhale. Relax your shoulders and other muscles. Do some type of physical movement to get your energy flowing as necessary. This could include some simple stretches, a yoga or tai chi movement, even a brief walk outside, or whatever works for you. Depending on your culture and belief system, you may also find it helpful to reflect on a verse, poem, or prayer.

Open the meeting in a manner that all feel comfortable with; perhaps even a moment of silence to quiet the busy mind and to engage the energy of the heart, not just the mind and ego. This type of centering must be done in a manner that is comfortable for the specific context and people involved. If it feels awkward or artificially imposed, the intent to begin with centering could easily have the opposite unintended negative impact of closing down people to authentic communication.

This preparation and centering is essential to a successful restorative dialogue process. Contemplative practice and mindfulness allow one to tap into an inner reservoir of strength, compassion, and wisdom that can foster the deepest expressions of unconditional love, forgiveness, and reconciliation. Contemplative practice and mindfulness provide practical tools to

Restorative Dialogue: A Path to Healing the Wounds

"shift gears," from ego-centered cognitive analysis and assessment to heart-centered presence and deep listening that is grounded in a spirit of humility and compassion. In doing so, the deepest level of learning and wisdom is accessed. The path towards forgiveness, centered in mindfulness and contemplative practice, is found in restorative dialogue among those closest to us, as well as in broader community conflict situations.

Practicing Restorative Dialogue with Those Close to Us

Conflict that periodically develops among friends and family can often create a permanent wedge between people or even destroy relationships. When using restorative dialogue as a safe process to address how the conflict is affecting the lives of all involved, it can actually lead to strengthening the relationships and repairing the harm of the conflict.

In building more healthy communication or in responding to specific conflicts that develop within families, whether between partners or between parents and children, people can benefit from restorative dialogue in very immediate and practical ways. For example, conducting weekly "family meetings" between parents and young children can be a highly effective way of checking in with each other about important things happening in each other's lives or surfacing specific problems that need to be addressed. Simply sitting at a table with the adult parents doing most of the talking is not likely to facilitate an open and honest exchange.

On the other hand, using the practices of a talking circle and deep listening can lead to healthy communication in which the kids feel safe enough to open up, since the parents are intentionally trying to limit being verbally dominant. Giving children the option to choose a talking piece important to them can help foster trust in the process. For example, in one case the children chose their favorite teddy bear as the talking piece and all family members respected that only the person who held the teddy bear was to speak.

Practicing Restorative Dialogue in Our Larger Community

So much of our life is spent in the larger community in which we reside and in our workplace where conflict is frequently present. In some cases, workplace conflict can be highly toxic, zapping the energy and organizational commitment of those hooked in the conflict. Restorative dialogue can shift the energy of organizational conflict from the frequent presence of passive and/or aggressive communication that leads to conflict escalation and personal stress enhancement to open communication of the harm experienced, the emotional and physical impact on all involved, and the yearning for conflict resolution and healing.

For example, a conflict between two nurses in a large urban hospital was resolved through restorative dialogue facilitated by a nurse manager that both trusted. In addition to conflict over specific work assignment responsibilities, the non-American cultural context of one of the nurses contributed to the conflict. The nurse manager knew that if this conflict was not dealt with directly it would affect the culture of the entire unit through implicit negative communication. The manager had each nurse meet with her separately in a location with few interruptions and enough time to not be rushed. She invited each nurse to separately tell her perspective of the conflict and how it was affecting her work performance and stress. The nurse manager then facilitated a joint meeting between the two conflicted nurses and set a tone of safety and respect in which both nurses would have time to tell their stories, express their feelings, and directly contribute to developing a plan to resolve the conflict. In the meeting, the session began with a few brief comments by the nurse manager and then an invitation to each nurse to tell the other how she perceived the conflict.

Conflict among neighbors or others within the communities in which we live often leads to further estrangement and even costly lawsuits. As with workplace conflicts, restorative dialogue can shift the energy of community conflict from the frequent presence of passive-aggressive communication that leads to conflict escalation and personal stress enhancement, to open communication of the harm experienced, the emotional and physical impact on all involved, and the yearning for conflict resolution and healing.

For example, a conflict developed at a local church in which allegations were made that one of the ushers was stealing cash from the collection plate. The accused usher was part of a recently arrived refugee family from Africa. Only the staff of the church knew of this allegation. The minister contacted a member of the congregation who was active in the restorative justice movement. It was decided that the circle process would be most effective in giving all involved an opportunity to talk about the conflict and how they felt. A co-facilitator from with an African cultural background was engaged. Following separate preparation of the involved parties a joint meeting was held. After two hours, all present left with a feeling of resolution and healing, which was felt beyond those present and had a positive impact for the larger congregational community.

Why Is It Important?

Interpersonal and intergroup conflict is an ever-present reality of human existence. These conflicts can be found among friends, co-workers, within families and communities, among politicians, and particularly between conflicting cultures and faith traditions. At a time when the manner in which conflict is addressed has become increasingly polarized and dysfunctional, restorative dialogue provides an opportunity for a safe, respectful, and effective process to address the conflict. Restorative dialogue fosters both accountability and healing.

The short examples provided above are witness to the power of restorative dialogue as a process to repair relationships and open doors to a greater sense of healing, peace, and forgiveness. Instead of avoiding the conflict and encouraging continued passive-aggressive, indirect communication among the involved parties, restorative dialogue provides a healthy outlet for release of the energy that drives conflict. The very personal stories offered more in depth in the following chapters of this book provide valuable lessons about healing and forgiveness from those who have experienced restorative dialogue in many diverse settings: in response to crime and violence, within families, and in schools, workplaces, and communities.

PART 1
Forgiveness for Victims of Crime

CHAPTER 3

A Burglary Leads to a Lasagna Meal

MANY YEARS AGO, MUCH earlier in his career, Mark was involved in a restorative justice program that he helped set up, in which victims of common property offenses, such as theft or burglary or vandalism, were given the opportunity to meet the young person or young adult who was responsible for this harm. The process was totally voluntary. In those early years there were only a handful of restorative justice programs throughout the country. Today there are many hundreds of such programs throughout the world. One case particularly stands out to Mark. It was one of his earliest experiences within his professional life of bearing witness to the enormous power of the energetic release of toxic emotional energy.

The Smith's home had been burglarized by a young man, Steve, who was twenty, while they were gone for the weekend. The neighbors called them when the police arrived. Mr. and Mrs. Smith traveled back south to their home in the city, from their cabin in the country. They did not have peace or reconciliation on their mind as they drove home. They were furious. Mr. Smith was an insurance agent. He frequently dealt with clients who were filing claims for burglary and other crimes. The young offender, Steve, was arrested. He admitted his guilt, and the judge, before sentencing him, referred him to a restorative justice program called Victim Offender Mediation. Carol, a person who worked with the program and was trained in the field, initiated the process. She first met with the offender before even contacting the victims, to check out if Steve, the offender, truly owned up to what he had done and was willing to enter a mediation process, to talk about what happened and to develop a plan to repair the harm. Steve was, although he had many reservations about it. In fact, he was very angry. He felt the victims, the Smiths, were ripping him off. He felt they were claiming far more restitution than for the items he actually took. Steve's anger was essentially used as an additional motivational factor for why he might want to consider talking with the Smiths, to talk about that openly and to work out a mutually agreed upon plan to repair the harm. Eventually Steve did agree to meet.

Before Carol, the mediator, went on to call and hopefully meet with the Smiths, she contacted Mark in the office. She talked about her concern, about Steve's high level of anger, which was fairly unusual with the offenders, who are usually pretty passive once they are caught in the system. She wondered if she should even proceed, yet Mark encouraged her to not let the anger of Steve be an obstacle. Carol called the Smiths, listened to their concerns, tried to set up a meeting with them face-to-face wherever they would prefer. Mr. Smith had answered the phone and he was extremely angry. He would refer to this "stupid punk" who broke into his home. He talked about how he had been ripped off two times before and it's probably the same idiot that did it again. He couldn't even listen to the few things that Carol was saying about the program. But eventually he learned a little bit about it and he said, "Well, let me give it a little more thought, and call me back next week."

Carol called him back the following week and he, in a somewhat hesitating voice, said, "Aw, yeah, I think I do want to hear more about it. My wife Sue will be with me. Why don't you come out to our home and we'll be glad to tell you more about how it affected us, and we want to learn more about the program." So Carol, the mediator, went out to their home, did a lot of deep listening, and slowly explained the program in a gentle and down-to-earth way. Eventually Mr. Smith said, "Yeah, I do, I want to tell that punk what it's like to be victimized; what it's like to have all your stuff taken." His wife, Sue, said, "Well, I know my husband wants to do this, but I don't want to do it, so he'll do it by himself." When Carol got back to the office the next day, she checked in with Mark and asked for his assistance. She said, "Mark, this case involves such a high level of anger from both the victim and offender. Can you help with this and co-facilitate?" Mark told Carol, "Sure, but do check in with both people to let them know that I'll be coming into the process and to make sure they feel comfortable with that, so there's no surprises." She did so and both the offender and the victims were okay with Mark being a co-facilitator.

A Burglary Leads to a Lasagna Meal

Mr. Smith indicated that he preferred having the mediation at a local library conference room in his neighborhood. When they came together at the library with Steve, it was a very tense and awkward moment. They all met each other in the hallway initially. Mrs. Smith was with her husband. The mediators weren't expecting that. Mrs. Smith said, "I know you weren't thinking I'd be here, but I came along to drag my husband out of it. I'm afraid he could lose it and get really nasty." So that kind of upped the concern of the co-mediators, Carol and Mark. But they proceeded. There were no handshakes, and only some brief verbal introductions. They went into the room that had been previously arranged for the mediation session. It was a huge room with no tables and the mediators really wanted tables for people to sit around to have some clear boundaries, but they all had to sit in just an open circle.

The co-mediator, Carol, did a nice job of giving the opening statement and talking about what they'd be doing that evening, inviting their participation, and thanking them for coming to the meeting. Mark added a few comments about if they need to take a break, just let them know, because they could do so at any time. Then Mark opened up the process by turning to Mr. Smith and inviting him to speak directly to Steve about how he felt about what happened. After Mr. Smith had finished, Mark used his body language of moving his hand from Mr. Smith to Steve, the offender, letting him know he could begin telling his story. Steve needed a little prompting. He was rocking in the chair, arms folded on his chest. He glared at the carpet, looking like he had no interest whatsoever in being there. The energy of Mr. Smith's presence was full of anger. In fact, within four minutes the anger got so high, with him calling Steve a punk, that Mark was just about ready to intervene and redirect the conversation, to essentially break the energy of his explosiveness and ask Steve to share his story. But before doing that, Steve actually was getting so agitated by this that he jumped out of his seat and he said, "Aw, this is a bunch of shit. I shouldn't have come." Mark jumped out of his chair, looked at Steve and said, "Steve, I can understand you wanting to go. Mr. Smith is very angry, but I know that he and his wife are here because they want to learn more about what happened. They want to learn more about you and they want to see if some plan to repair the harm can be worked out that seems fair. Can you give it a few more minutes, and then if it's just not working, go ahead and leave?" That appeared to be enough to validate Steve's anger and to encourage him to stick around awhile.

This was truly the beginning of Mark's learning of the healing power of releasing toxic emotional energy in conflicts. The outburst of anger by both Steve and Mr. Smith was probably the most pivotal moment in the entire mediation session. It was a transformative moment. Their body language was stiff, and their voice tones were high and intense. But after the verbal explosion of their emotional energy, they both sat up a little more erect, and their tones of voice was significantly lower. Mr. Smith began asking Steve questions in a very direct way. Steve actually looked at him, rather than staring down at the carpet as before.

As incredible as this might sound, after about forty-five minutes there were some moments of silence in the midst of the Smiths telling their story and Steve telling his. Moments of silence. Then Mr. Smith leaned toward his wife who was sitting a little behind him and they whispered. Carol and Mark were wondering what in the world was going on. But they didn't interrupt. They honored the process and bore witness to what was going on, because the co-mediators sensed, at an intuitive level, something very powerful was happening. After they whispered to each other, Mr. Smith looked at Steve, bent over close to him, and in a soft voice tone said, "Do you know our daughter Sara?" Steve said, "Yeah." Mr. Smith said, "Was she involved in this? I mean, did she set you guys up to hit our place?" Steve said, "No, Sara's a good kid. She was not involved at all." Mr. Smith leaned back toward his wife and they whispered again, and then he turned and looked straight at Steve, leaned forward even more closely and in a softer voice said, "Do you ever see Sara? Ever since she ran from that drug treatment program, we haven't seen her for the last year and a half." Steve responded, "Yeah, I see her every now and then." Now Mr. Smith, the angry, furious victim looked at Steve, the criminal, the convicted felon and said, "Next time you see Sara, could you tell her that her mom and dad really love her? We miss her. And tell her we'd love her to come home."

The co-mediators were bearing witness to the most incredible energetic shift in major conflict that they had ever witnessed up to that time. The energy of anger, hostility, and dehumanizing of the other person, which was present at the beginning, and the energy of tension and awkwardness, had now shifted to a very different, gentler form of energetic communication, in which the victims were seeking help in their parenting from the crook. It was a process of mutual aid; a very old social work concept. Steve was no longer the convicted felon, the burglar. He was a guy that messed up, and who was at some level connected with their daughter from who

A Burglary Leads to a Lasagna Meal

they were estranged. They needed and wanted Steve to perhaps help them reconnect with their daughter, Sara.

The session went on, and they eventually got to talking about the actual losses that the Smiths experienced. They brought a list of damages and items that were stolen. It was given to Steve. When Steve looked at it, he stiffened up and he said, "No, I took the TV, the VCR, the stereo set, and some of these items, but I really did not take these other items." Mr. Smith said, "Yes, you did, they're all gone." And Steve said, "No I didn't." And Mr. Smith said, "Yes, you did." And this went back and forth.

The co-mediators became increasingly concerned that all of the good energy that had been felt prior to this part of the conversation might be eliminated. So Mark interrupted and said, "Hang on, let me just check out something. Steve, was it Friday night that you broke into the Smith's home?" Steve said, "Yeah." And Mark looked at Mr. Smith and asked, "Was it Sunday night that you and your wife came back?" And he said, "Yeah." Mark then asked Steve, "Did you tell any of your buddies about what you did, about breaking into this place?" And he said, "Yeah, actually, I had a few beers and I was telling them how easy it was to break into this place. It was, like, around one o'clock in the morning Friday night." Mark looked at Mr. Smith and said, "You know, I don't know if this could have happened, but is it possible that one of Steve's buddies came back and took some other stuff?" The Smiths whispered to each other and then Mr. Smith said, "Well, maybe that is what happened. Steve seems to be sincere about owning up to what he took. Let's just talk about what he admits to." They went on to talking more about the losses and developed an actual plan to repair the harm, for which Steve would repay the monetary loss that the Smiths incurred in specific monthly payments over a year-and-a-half period of time.

It was a very specific, clear restitution agreement. At the end of the agreement, as things were wrapping up, the co-mediators could sense the energy of the group was diminishing, so Mark said before closing, "You know, in cases like this, where it's a more severe case, and where there's quite a bit of monetary restitution, we really encourage a follow-up meeting at your convenience. Just to check out things and if there's any problems to renegotiate or adjust it in any way possible to make sure the agreement's completed. What do you think about that?" The Smiths talked with each other. Steve was giving it some thought, and the Smiths said, "Yeah, that's okay." Then Steve looked at the co-mediators and said, "Mark, I think that would be a good idea. Could we have the meeting at my house?" And then he looked at the Smiths and he said, "You know, I'm not a burglar. I mean, what I did was wrong, I broke into your house, but I'm not some criminal. I'd like you to come to my house and meet my wife and meet my little baby." Steve looked at the Smiths again, and, no kidding, he said, "Do you guys like lasagna? I'm a real good lasagna cook." The co-mediators were thinking, wow, incredible. The meeting ended with a few comments by co-mediators, and as they all were walking out, it was clear that the energy had shifted in a huge way.

If an empirical instrument was available that could clearly measure energy, it can be asserted with tremendous confidence that you would have seen enormously thick, toxic, tense, awkward energy, closed energy, at the beginning, and you would have seen that transform over the two-hour period to the ending, where the energy was really light, open, receptive, and full of connection among people. Walking out to the parking lot, Steve forgot about the co-mediators. He and the Smiths were talking with each other and the Smiths were asking him about his child's name and how old she was. They were just talking like neighbors, like human beings.

A follow-up conversation with both the Smiths and Steve, quite a few months afterward, validated again the power of this mediation session. The Smiths experienced the power of facing this conflict, moving beyond the fears, the stereotypes, the demonizing, and looking at the humanity within the very person who angered them so much. Steve also looked deeply at the humanity in the people he victimized; that the Smiths were not targets, but were people who had hopes and dreams and family needs and were deeply affected by what had happened in their home. It was precisely again in facing the conflict directly that all of the parties found a level of peace they would never have experienced going through the conventional criminal justice system.

CHAPTER 4

A Tragic Car Crash Gives Way to Reconciliation

RICHARD, A LOCAL BUSINESSMAN and a single father of a four-year-old girl, had spent the day drinking beer with his buddies at the county fair in northern California. But when the rain came, he rushed for his full-sized Chevy pick-up truck in the parking lot, along with many other wet fairgoers. In a drunken fog, Richard became frustrated with the long line of cars and pushed the accelerator down as he swerved to the left in order to shoot past the other automobiles.

Anne and her husband of fourteen years, Jim, were walking on the right side of the road and in the direct path of Richard's two-ton truck. In his intoxicated rush, the off-duty police officer hit the couple, who up until this moment had lived ordinary middle-class lives. Without ever seeing them, Richard injured Anne and killed Jim. He didn't stop, didn't even realize what he had done. Only later, when he heard the call on his police radio, did he understand the gravity of his actions.

Richard confessed, and in due course, the former police officer would be convicted of negligent homicide and sentenced to three years of incarceration.

Eighteen months after the incident, Anne was referred to a restorative justice program in her community. She had a desire to talk with the man who had killed her husband, to find out who did this, and what he was thinking. She wanted to let him know the devastating impact this had on her life.

From the start, the restorative dialogue facilitator sensed the energy of anger and impatience from Anne. He listened to her story and the emotional intensity of her loss, then began slowly introducing the process of restorative dialogue in the context of victim-offender trauma, talking about

PART 1—FORGIVENESS FOR VICTIMS OF CRIME

how there would need to be a good deal of separate preparation. The facilitator would need to connect with Richard in prison, as well. It could be many months before a meeting could occur, and the meeting might not ever occur. It was very possible that either Richard or Anne would get to a point in the process at which each would change his or her mind about meeting with the other, and for the process to move forward, both parties needed to agree to meet.

"This is a voluntary process, not something you force a prisoner to do," explained the facilitator. Anne's impatience was urgent and clear: "I want to meet with this guy *now*! I don't need any preparation. I've lost my husband. My life is in turmoil. I have to meet this *punk*. I don't know why I have to meet him, but I just know I've got to meet with him to free myself."

The initial conversation with Anne set in motion many months of groundwork, including several face-to-face preparation meetings with her and with Richard. Many phone conversations were involved.

The joint session began with a gentle opening statement inviting Anne to share with Richard her story of the impact of this crime on her life, without any interruptions, and then he would have the same chance to share his perspective. Later, if they wanted, they could discuss any thoughts about repairing the harm, in whatever way, perhaps even symbolic.

Again, the spirit of impatience arose. Anne interrupted, "Look, I'm not here to tell stories or listen to stories. I've got questions for this punk." She stood up from her chair, breathing heavily, "I just want to talk with this guy."

The facilitator looked at Richard, "Are you okay with just jumping into this and getting going?"

"Yeah, that's okay. I'm here to help her out in whatever way I can," he replied.

Anne was a large woman and even when both were standing she was taller than Richard, an average-sized white male. Still looming, with the tone and posture of an aggressive prosecutor, Anne would point at Richard and repeatedly ask, "Why the hell did you do this? Didn't you give any thought to this? You're a cop. Of all people you should know you don't drive the way you were, and then leave the scene of an accident. How the hell could you have done this?" She asked all kinds of other questions, too.

Richard responded as best he could. He talked about what led up to the tragedy, and how he'd never had any issue with drinking and driving before. He said he couldn't believe what he did and that he ran from the

A Tragic Car Crash Gives Way to Reconciliation

scene. He talked about how ashamed he was, how he had thoughts of killing himself, and how he held a gun to his head the night it happened.

Anne and Richard continued talking for more than an hour and then Anne requested a break. Before leaving the room, she surprised the facilitator with a request, "I really want to talk directly with Richard by myself. I want to talk to him; just the two of us." The facilitator looked to Richard and reassured him that he did not have to do this, but he wanted to do it, too. As a very experienced facilitator of restorative dialogue, he agreed to this and waited in the attached room, chatting with a friend of Anne's who drove her to the meeting. Through the thin door he could hear the occasional noise. After another a half, the door opened, and Anne walked in. Her energy was entirely different. She slowly shuffled into the room, with her head down, breathing slowly, offering no comments.

Anne slouched in a chair near the facilitator. "He's not a punk. He killed my Jim, but he's not a punk." And after a few more moments of silence she looked up again and said, "I can't believe what I just did before coming in here. Richard and I had talked about everything . . . and there's this moment of silence . . . and I looked up at Richard and I said, I can't believe I did this, I said, 'Do you need a hug?' . . . And he said, 'Yeah,' with tears in his eyes."

And she went over and hugged this man, who up to then was a punk, the monster who killed her husband.

The facilitator went on and debriefed a bit more, most of which was not verbal; it was just being present with Anne, with her totally relaxed energy, just as he had been present with her angry, impatient energy. Her body posture, her tone of voice, and her breathing pattern were powerful indicators that something energetic had shifted in a big way. Before she had twitched and gasped. Now she was relaxed, calm, and spoke with a soft tone of voice.

The facilitator then went in and sat down next to Richard, who was still in his chair, almost in a meditative mood, saying nothing, very relaxed, very peaceful. He asked Richard if he had any regrets about being left alone with Anne.

"No, we needed to talk with each other. You have been helpful, but frankly, even before the break we forgot you were there. She needed to let me know the pain I caused in her life, and it was not easy hearing it. I've never felt more powerful feelings of shame within myself in my life." And then, referring to the hug, he said, "I can't believe what we did at the end."

CHAPTER 5

A Mother Goes to Prison to Get Some Answers

Surviving the death of a child is inconceivable to many people who have never had to experience such a loss. In Bridget's case, coping after loss was even more difficult when her only child was senselessly murdered by another young man for no apparent reason. More than a decade later, Bridget reflected on what happened one tragic evening and her process of healing over many years. While Bridget didn't aspire to forgive her son's murderer, her experience offers insight into walking in the energy of forgiveness and letting go of hate in your heart.

On July 3, 2002, Bridget was enjoying the evening at a friend's home to barbeque and watch a Minnesota Twins game when she received a call from Brad, a friend of her twenty-two-year-old son D. J. She knew D. J. had joined friends for an outdoor music festival as part of the annual Fourth of July celebration in St. Paul. Brad told Bridget something had happened to D. J. and she needed to come to the hospital. Bridget asked what was wrong and Brad said he didn't know, but she should just come. At the time, Bridget wasn't too concerned, since D. J. had a way of getting himself hurt and it hadn't been her first time seeing him in an emergency room for a minor injury. Her friend offered to go with, and while Bridget said he didn't need to, he decided to accompany her anyway.

Upon arriving at the hospital, Bridget approached a desk and gave a receptionist her name. The person at the desk asked her to wait, and shortly after that a nurse came out to talk with her. As the nurse addressed her and asked Bridget to come with her, Bridget noticed the nurse had a crucifix above her name badge. The nurse took her to a private room and asked her to wait for the doctor. Bridget was becoming concerned. Something didn't

A Mother Goes to Prison to Get Some Answers

feel right. When the doctor came in to talk with Bridget, he spoke in a bunch of medical terminology that she couldn't understand, until he ended with a very serious tone, stressing that D. J.'s condition was very serious.

The realization hit Bridget and she asked, "Do you mean he could die from this?" The doctor said yes. As Bridget was trying to comprehend all that was happening, she was now wondering: where were the friends who D. J. had been with; what had happened? To this day she still doesn't know all that happened that turned her life upside down on that July day. What she did know at the time was that D. J. had been punched, and his life was in jeopardy.

By ten PM, Bridget's sister, Dee, had arrived, and they were able to see D. J. for the first time. D. J. was in a coma and had many medical devices attached to him, but for the most part he looked fine. This was so confusing. Dee, who was a nurse, was paying attention to the various medical readings and charts, but didn't share any of it with Bridget. They stayed with D. J. in his hospital room, and brought him reminders of home in an attempt to communicate and support him. Bridget's other sister came from Kansas City to be with them also.

On Friday, July 5 an MRI was done and a doctor met with them to share the results. As the doctor gave them the news, that D. J.'s brain stem had been crushed, Bridget could see Dee's body slump over. From that moment, Bridget knew D. J. was going to die. The doctor said there was no chance for D. J. to come out of the coma. An extremely difficult decision about removing life support equipment needed to be made. Bridget tried to deny the seriousness of D. J.'s condition and questioned whether she could bring him home and take care of him. Ultimately she needed to face that her son was gone. On Sunday, they removed D. J. from life support and he died on the next Wednesday, one week after he received the fatal blow.

Bridget was still in shock. How could this have happened? How could her only child, her son, be gone from such a senseless act as a single punch in the face? Roger, the person who was charged and sent to prison for the deadly blow, was about seventy-five pounds lighter than D. J., so it was inconceivable to Bridget that this could be the outcome. And why was D. J. even with Roger, a young man she had never met or heard of? What she learned in time was that two groups of young men, one being D. J. and his friends and the other being Roger and his friends, were at the festival. The groups crossed paths and a couple guys from each group exchanged verbal taunts. With that, Roger said to a member of his group, "You're not going to just let him punk you?" The kid didn't want to fight, but Roger did. Bridget's son D. J. spoke up from the other group, in defense of his smaller friend, saying that it wouldn't be a fair fight, to which Roger responded he would fight D. J. instead. According to witnesses, D. J. said he wouldn't throw the first punch, but was prepared to defend himself. Roger then threw a punch with such powerful force that D. J.'s body was thrown backward and he hit the ground headfirst, never to awaken.

The healing process for Bridget would be long. She had much gratitude for Survivor Resources, a nonprofit that assists helps of violent crime cope and grieve. A friend knew of the organization and recommended that Bridget attend a support group, which became her lifeline for many years. Her friend picked her up every Monday for three months, bringing her to the group. Along the way, Bridget decided she wanted to sit down face-to-face with her son's killer, who was now in prison.

When asked why she wanted to meet Roger, Bridget said ever since she saw him in the courtroom she felt compelled to talk with him. "There were three court hearings and while our family was together in the room, I noticed the only one there for Roger was his attorney—no one else. I wondered why. The sentencing was different; there were all kinds of people. I wanted to see his parents, but when I asked where they were, I was told they weren't there. Then after reading impact statements, the judge said something that hit me. The judge said you couldn't have two kids coming from such different lives." Roger had been taken from his mother for the last time when he was eleven and had been in foster care ever since. "I just thought, this kid hasn't been hugged. I wanted to know, what could be in him that he could punch another kid so hard as to kill him, when they only knew each other for fifteen minutes? I wanted to know if this could be the reason my child is no longer with me—because his mother and father didn't parent him," Bridget explained. When Roger was escorted from the courtroom to go to prison, he looked at Bridget and said, "I'm so sorry." Bridget wanted to know, "What was he sorry for? For my son's death? For what?"

Four years later, after much preparation, Bridget was ready to face her son's killer. Before the meeting with Roger, Bridget went in ready to break him down, to hurt him and to push him to want to change, break him down to turn him around. Looking back, she talks about being prepared with ammunition, such as Mother's Day cards, pictures, and other important items that symbolized her relationship with her son and all that had been taken from them.

A Mother Goes to Prison to Get Some Answers

When first sitting down face-to-face, Roger asked Bridget how he should address her, and she told him, "Miss Gibson." He asked, "Can I call you Bridget?" And she repeated, "No, it's Miss Gibson." "I wanted him to tell me what happened, everything that day, that led him to go to this extreme," Bridget said. But Roger answered it wasn't from anything that day. He just wanted to fight. Roger explained that 95 percent of his aggression toward D. J. was rage from his childhood, while just 5 percent was about the actual situation involving D. J.

Bridget went into the meeting angry, but as they talked her insight grew, and she left instead wanting to parent Roger and to see him be a better person. Bridget told him that she was sorry he didn't get the love he needed from his parents. Bridget felt emotionally spent after the visit. "The whole meeting with Roger helped me to move on with the grieving process, because all of my questions were answered," Bridget said.

When Bridget is asked about whether she forgives Roger, she declares no. She explains, "To use the word *forgiveness* feels like letting him off the hook, and I don't want him off the hook. I want him on the hook for this for the rest of his life. I think he can live a life of worth and goodness and that's the best way of meeting his maker. I don't think it's from me that he needs forgiveness. So is it forgiveness or kindness?"

Yet, as Bridget speaks, a tone of compassion and concern is heard in her voice. Even though Bridget doesn't forgive per se, she does wish for Roger to have a good life. She said, "Someday he may have a family and when he holds his own baby, he will know that's what he took from me. I told him he needs to be a really good father. Many of D. J.'s friends wanted revenge. "They wanted Roger dead, but I told them no," says Bridget. She let them know she expected them to follow and respect her way of handling the situation.

Eleven years after the murder of her son, compassion and kindness are what Bridget most expresses for Roger, while still expecting accountability for his actions. Bridget says, "I think it's more like walking in the spirit of forgiveness. I walk with kindness and care for him, but still holding strong expectations. I don't hold a grudge. I've seen people so strapped with hate. I will work with people to let go of hate."

Bridget may not use the word *forgiveness* or believe it's her who needs to forgive the killer of her son, yet the energy of forgiveness is present. For Bridget, walking in the spirit of forgiveness, the responsibility and accountability for her son's murder is still on Roger. But knowing his story, Bridget can have compassion and not let deep anger and pain prevent her from continuing on with peace in her heart.

CHAPTER 6

A Woman Connects with Her Father's Murderer

When Pam went through a three-hour-long restorative dialogue encounter with the man who murdered her father, she herself was truly amazed by how much relief it brought her. Having unanswered questions answered and hearing genuine remorse on the part of the offender allowed, in her own words, a "cleansing to happen." By way of contrast, her feelings of intense anger and mistrust at the start of the two-year restorative process were very evident to the two facilitators who initially met with her. Even on the morning of the scheduled dialogue meeting in prison, after lots of good preparation with Pam, the facilitators felt nervous about how the conversation might go. Would she be able to handle this situation of coming face-to-face with the offender? Would they have to cut the conversation short for the good of both of them?

According to Pam, the quality of preparation made all the difference in the world. It is true that her troubled and negative feelings were still active within her at the time of sitting down at the table for a restorative dialogue. But Jack, the offender who was serving twenty-five years in prison, was also on a journey toward something good, toward personal change and freedom. He carried a long history of anger and pent-up pain, which had ultimately exploded in the episode of the murder. Being in prison gave him the necessary time to think about his past and to get reoriented in his thinking. In the end, this victim and offender encounter allowed both Pam and Jack to connect on a heart-to-heart level, and it became very meaningful to both of them. How is it, then, that such intense feelings of anger and personal pain could feed into a process that in the end yielded deep compassion and understanding? Specifically, how was Pam able to handle her own feelings in this face-to-face setting? Did some form of forgiveness happen that day?

Reflecting back on her process years later, Pam said she experienced a "moment of grace" that allowed her to handle her feelings in a way where she was in control of them rather than her feelings being in control of her. Forgiveness, for Pam, is not a matter of getting "over" your feelings and moving on in life. From her perspective, hard feelings cannot be neatly tied up into a little package and put aside as if you are done with them. Instead, forgiveness is being able, over time, to honestly have hard feelings without acting on them. She recognized how the meeting with Jack allowed for elements of forgiveness to happen that were like gifts to her. Her chance to tell her story in full, his chance to apologize, her chance to have questions answered and to learn about his past, and his chance to understand her and gain more compassion, was all part of bridge-building. From this activity came "pieces of forgiveness" for Pam, even though she could not simply forgive Jack for what he did. We will come back to this paradox later.

The story of the death of Pam's father is a very tragic one. At a point where her family trusted Jack as someone to help out during the holiday season, an episode happened in the kitchen with just Jack and Pam's father present. With uncontrollable rage, Jack beat the father on his head from behind and then brutally stabbed him forty times. Fleeing the house with stolen possessions and a checkbook, he left a thick trail of evidence that made the court trial, one year later, incontestable. Pam, along with her family members, was grief-struck and angry. She was fortunate to receive good support from a therapist known for helping police officers, and from a homicide victims' support group.

Nearly twenty years after the initial crime, Pam learned about the restorative justice option for victims of serious and violent crimes. At her own initiative she pursued the opportunity to meet with the perpetrator of her father's death. Understandably, trust issues were huge for her when facing the lead facilitator for the first time. She had already been with many therapists who, in her words, "had a look of horror on their face, rather than a look of empathy and understanding." When telling her story once again, the last thing she wanted was to feel hurt again. But the two restorative justice facilitators provided a sense of empathy and understanding that helped her gain new trust. This was all the more important, as one of the facilitators recalled how Pam's body language and word choices spoke of more anger than the content of what she said verbally. This facilitator, over years of experience, had never before seen such a high level of anger and intensity in a victim client. Without question, this foundation of trust, along with many layers of good preparation, were essential in helping Pam transform the toxic emotional energy she was still carrying within her into a new life energy to help her move forward.

In a video interview done after the meeting with Jack, Pam recalled the many ways in which she was well prepared before coming to the joint meeting. The facilitators met with her about a half a dozen times, interspersing those meetings with separate meetings with Jack in prison. This allowed, with permission, information about Jack's readiness to be passed on to Pam in successive bits. Things that would be said or questions that would be asked were all placed "on the table" in a way to diminish any unexpected surprises. At the same time, Pam recounted how she was not led to have high hopes for what would come out of meeting with Jack. The facilitators prepared her with low expectations, and thus she knew that any other positive outcomes would be a gift to her. This two years of preparation also gave Pam the time to know if she really wanted to go through with the meeting.

Along with touring the prison ahead of time, one very important preparatory exercise was for Pam to write down every question she wanted to ask Jack when they would meet. The court trial did not allow for all questions to be aired, since it mostly revolved around the defense attorney's agenda. Over several weeks, Pam kept adding more and more questions to her list, things that lacked closure and had been bothering her for years like ghosts in her mind seeking a final resting place. She recalled how writing the list had a lot of value by itself. "That alone was a healing process for me, to look at this and see how much I was carrying around. And it may not get resolved, but I'm going to try."

This list of questions, with Pam's permission, was then shared with Jack, who in turn shared a list of questions back with Pam. It was a powerful way to build trust before even meeting together. In a sense, a violent crime robs a person of a positive energy of trust. Pam knew that "you are never the same" after being impacted by the murder of a loved one. "You'll never trust others the same way as you did before." For this reason, the restorative process, hard as it is at first, works to create a credit of trust that can fill an existing debit of trust. This new credit of trust, aided by the relationship with the facilitators, can later be drawn upon in finding trust with the other party.

One of the biggest lingering questions for Pam was, "Once he gets out of prison, will he come and hurt me or my family?" The force of this concern can be felt in the context of the original crime, which involved Jack's unpredictable explosion of anger and rage. Even though Pam felt very prepared for the visit and felt comfortable with the facilitator and her husband who was present for support, this concern about Jack hurting someone again was very palpable to her. In her mind, however, she was already able to live with the tension between wanting him dead and wanting something profoundly good to come out of the meeting for both her and him. These two things did not cancel each other out; they coexisted in her mind.

The day finally came for her, after a two-hour drive, to meet with Jack in the prison. Both facilitators and Pam's husband were there as supports. Looking back, the most helpful thing that happened was for her lingering questions to get answered, every one of them. One question had to do with a matter about Pam's father who, according to the defense attorney, provoked Jack. This scenario was also printed in the newspapers. Jack, however, was able to explain exactly what happened, giving more truth than what came out in the legal process. To know that her father had not done as the attorney had said greatly helped Pam. In addition to getting answers, it was also very helpful for Pam to talk through the countless impacts to herself and the family, and she noted how this had a twofold benefit. First, it was good for her to recapture the entire story and tell it to Jack in a way that validated how hard the impacts truly were. Second, it was good to see Jack's reaction to hearing the whole story and respond in a genuine way. During the trial, he seemed unresponsive, showing no emotion. This time he was more open and understanding and that made a huge difference for Pam.

Far beyond what Pam had initially expected, the three-hour meeting created a space for listening, sharing, honesty, understanding, and assurance, all of which amounted to a deeper connection that would have seemed unimaginable to her in earlier years. "We looked each other in the eye and just talked." A high point of the conversation came when Jack said to Pam, "I will never hurt you or a member of your family." He wanted her to know that, plain and simple, and this exchange was a big moment for both of them. At another point Pam asked Jack to talk about his childhood, and while it was hard for him to name the sources of his anger, it became evident to Pam that Jack was "a victim of his own life." He even said that it had been just a matter of time before he would have killed someone. "Hearing this truth was healing for me," said Pam. She knew it was no longer about her father but about Jack's pain. In a strange way, this gave her more compassion for him.

PART 1—Forgiveness for Victims of Crime

Pam felt that if Jack had made no apology, it would have been very sad. But Jack apologized over and over for different ways that Pam and her family had been affected, and she knew he wasn't faking it. To her "it was a gift." But she also recognized that "it was a gift for both of us. It also unburdened him, too." Jack's sorrow for what he did was real, and Pam could sense this. At the same time it was clear to Pam that Jack had suffered much internally for what he had done, and this also led her to feel sorrow for him. "That sounds terrible," she later reflected, "but that helped me to see he was a human being and not a monster." Altogether, this encounter amounted to an enormous shift of emotional energy from intense toxic anger and pain to an equally strong sense of release and goodwill.

On leaving the prison that day, Pam experienced a set of feelings that were very memorable. "I felt so much relief, as if a cleansing had happened. My questions had been answered and I was jubilant that I wouldn't have to worry any more." She also felt degrees of sadness; sadness for the family loss, sadness for Jack's life, and even sadness that she had not done this dialogue earlier. Pam said, "It would have reduced years of worrying about all this stuff!" Part of the paradox in Pam's experience was that there was a very real sense of journeying forward and not being stuck in the feelings of her past, and yet she also had a very real sense of owning her feelings and not wanting to disregard them by moving on. It was as if her feelings, born out of her experience as a victim, could be traded in for something that was meaningful to her.

When asked about whether her experience with Jack involved forgiveness, Pam reflected the same paradox in how she dealt with her feelings. "The murder is not mine to forgive; there are some things that are unforgiveable. He shouldn't even be breathing right now." On the other hand, Pam described her encounter with Jack as "a moment of grace" that allowed for connection and compassion to grow for both of them. "It seemed like God had a hand in it." Are these contradictory perspectives? This tension makes perfect sense to Pam, "if you are comfortable with who you are and with your emotions." What it really came down to was her recognition that feelings stemming from the death of a loved one just don't go away or get neatly resolved. It is not a matter of whether you have the feelings or whether you move on in life; it is a matter of how you handle those feelings.

This orientation fits well with a rejection of forgiveness as a social expectation to "let bygones be bygones," or to say, "That's water under the bridge." Pam said that she didn't want the kind of peace where there is almost a pressure to forgive. In contrast, Pam sought elements of forgiveness that helped her heal not away from her feelings, but with and through her feelings. "I'm not going to change or mock how I feel so that others can feel comfortable with it, or others can say, 'Oh good, she's able to let it go.'" Instead, she visualizes her feelings in a box that is placed on a shelf in her closet, and whenever she wants to take that box down and open it up, she knows that it is "okay" to have a "bad night." "That doesn't mean I'm a bad person for feeling what I feel, and it doesn't mean that because I don't forgive Jack that I've done something wrong or haven't completed my process." Rather, it means to her that she can handle things as she chooses to handle them, knowing well that she will not act on these feelings in hurtful ways. Significantly, the restorative dialogue process was a key aid in her personal growth to control her feelings, though earlier therapy also set her in this same direction.

Even though the word *forgive* did not come into play in the restorative dialogue, it is clear that all that happened took place, as Pam phrased it, "along the lines of forgiveness." A true expression of this was the lean to a positive future. Toward the end of the meeting Pam told Jack that she bore no ill will toward him in the future, and that she wanted him to not hurt anyone else, but to be successful. Similarly, Pam's husband wished him the best, and assured Jack that no revenge of any sort would happen. These intentions for a positive future are hallmark signs of any act of forgiveness where people have shifted the focus from the past to the future.

Perhaps the most profound discovery for Pam was how her encounter with Jack led to her moment of being able to forgive herself. For years she felt somewhat at fault for her role in connecting Jack to her father. By meeting Jack face-to-face, and sensing firsthand his change of heart, this "moment of grace" gave her the therapeutic space to forgive herself by letting go of that inner weight. It may be that using the word *forgive* in this context confirms how real forgiveness can be when it comes to managing one's own feelings. This fits well with a concluding statement Pam made about Jack: "I'm not ready to forgive him, but I can say that I don't feel the same way I did before about him either. I feel very differently about him."

PART 2

Forgiveness for Families

CHAPTER 7

A Broken Family Comes Together

JAMES FERGUSON WAS FIRST exposed to restorative justice as a college student pursuing a law degree. He interned in the district attorney's office where he had the opportunity to see restorative justice applied and his interest in community-based restorative processes grew, so during law school he spent time learning the skill of facilitation and led restorative justice circles as well as victim-offender mediation sessions. After law school, James brought and applied restorative justice principles to his various work environments, facilitating circles in high schools and nonprofit organizations.

As James was building a successful career, however, he was noticing growing tensions on another front, within his family life. He decided something needed to be done. James's story demonstrates the power of restorative processes in a family context, and one family's inspiring journey with the energy of forgiveness.

James has a big family: two brothers, five sisters, parents, in-laws, nieces, and nephews, which means there's plenty of room for misunderstandings and conflict to develop. Family members seemed to confide in James, so he knew a lot about what was going on behind the scenes that other family members didn't know. Because of his standing as the trusted confidant in the family, James could see the family was reaching a point of real crisis. Individuals and couples were experiencing serious challenges, but couldn't openly talk about their struggles.

For starters, one of James's sister had been suffering in silence in a toxic marriage for years, but was afraid to divorce for a number of reasons, of which one of the biggest was their mother's view of divorce. Their mother saw divorce as one of the worst evils a person could do to a family, so when James's sister finally decided to get a divorce, "all hell broke loose," James recalls.

Their mother couldn't understand how her daughter could put her family through the pain of divorce, and as a result, so much tension came between mother and daughter that the two stopped speaking to each other. This moreover drove a wedge between James's mother and father, since Dad was more supportive of James's sister. Mom was so upset at this, she threatened she might as well get a divorce also, given she felt there was so much disregard for her point of view. Anger and resentment continued to build.

Amidst this conflict, another sister was suffering in silence with her own life challenges. She had recently had a baby and was struggling with postpartum depression, but didn't have a safe space to talk about what she was going through. At the same time, one of James's brothers and sister-in-law were emotionally stressed from attempting to conceive a child and not having any success after two years of marriage. They had begun to undergo tests to determine any physiological reasons for their inability to conceive a child, and were both afraid they would learn that they would be incapable of having children altogether.

James recalls, "I was the only one who knew what family members were going through, and I didn't want to carry the load myself. I've always been interested in finding solutions to problems, and for my family I wanted to find a safe space to bring everyone together." As a family, they had hit rock bottom. People no longer wanted to come to family functions and weren't talking to each other. James decided it was time to talk with his dad about the situation, and find resolution. His dad agreed it was time to bring people together to attempt to mend family relationships.

James believed the situation called for a circle dialogue process based on the principles of restorative justice he had learned and successfully applied in work situations. He approached his mother with the idea, and proposed that he would facilitate the family circle. He also asked his dad, and both said they were open to anything that could possibly work to bring everyone together. Prior to this, they had family meetings on occasion, which ended with everyone mad at each other and frustrated. Following the principles of a restorative dialogue circle, James was hopeful they could reach a different conclusion.

To prepare, James talked with everyone one-on-one to explain the process, hear their concerns, and make sure they were agreeable about participating. After talking to everyone, James carefully and thoughtfully

A Broken Family Comes Together

prepared questions to facilitate family members sharing in the circle. They came together for the circle, and James introduced everyone to the process, including guidelines to maintain a safe space for everyone, and the talking piece that would be passed around the circle, giving everyone a turn to talk freely without interruption. As they proceeded, he posed the first question to his family members: "What is your greatest fear right now?"

When the talking piece was passed to James's sister who had gotten a divorce, she took the time to express how difficult it was for her to decide to get a divorce. She had many fears and concerns, her greatest fear being the impact the divorce would have on her children. She felt a tremendous responsibility for them and was most afraid that her children would be negatively affected, and would truly hate her as a result. As she shared her truth, a change began to take place among family members, especially with James's mother.

"My mom could now see and understand that my sister did not take the decision to divorce lightly," explained James. "More tears were shed than at a funeral." James went on to say that what made the difference for family members in the circle is that everyone felt safe. "We all could see that solutions to our problems would come from our family being together," said James.

As the circle dialogue progressed, family members started to talk about how they could make things different moving forward. They decided to set up committees focused on various aspects of their family's health and well-being. James's brother who is a police officer and the most physically fit agreed to be the chair of a family health committee. The family decided to create a conflict mediation committee, which would be chaired by James, so the family had a structure and process in place to handle future conflicts in a safe and productive way. A family finance committee was established to make sure everyone's basic needs were met. A family social committee was created so that attention was given to the family having fun together and maintaining healthy relationships. And lastly, a committee was created for the grandchildren. James explained, "We wanted to make sure the same teachings and values we had were passed on to the kids, our next generation. Specifically we wanted to make sure the kids were able to experience our Christian upbringing and build strong relationships with each other, just as our generation had been able to do."

When asked what contributed to the success of the circle process to reunite his family, James said while he happened to be trained in restorative

PART 2—FORGIVENESS FOR FAMILIES

justice practices, what was most important was that he talked to everyone ahead of time and knew what was going on. He didn't want anyone to feel exposed or called out, so he put a lot of thought into preparation and developing the questions in a way that allowed everyone to feel safe.

When probed about the role of forgiveness in the process of his family conflict resolution, James explained, "We never used the word *forgiveness*, but you could still see it. We had a shift in energy. My mom in particular—she had so many things against my sister, but when she heard how much pain my sister had endured, Mom was aware of the pain she had pushed my sister to stay in. There's something powerful about restorative justice in circle dialogue, since there's more listening than talking." Forgiveness did indeed occur within James's family relationships, even though the word was not spoken.

CHAPTER 8

A Daughter Journeys from Incest to Healing

SOME OF THE MOST challenging conflicts or traumas to overcome occur within families. At times the abuse or conflict is so great that it impacts family members throughout their lives, without resolution. Such situations may evoke post-traumatic stress, physical health conditions, escalating conflict over the years, wedges between family members who will no longer talk to each other, and even acts of vengeance in an attempt to cause harm to those who have harmed others. The journey towards healing and forgiveness can be long and hard. Susan, a survivor of incest during her adolescence, experienced some of the worst things imaginable perpetrated by her own father. She was sexually abused for six years, between the ages of twelve and eighteen. Her healing journey reveals a tremendous amount of pain, but also a sense of hope that forgiveness and healing can occur in even the toughest of family victimization situations.

At eighteen years old, Susan was graduating from high school and leaving her family for the first time to attend college. It wasn't until she left her parent's home that her father stopped sexually abusing her. While not usually the case in incest victimization, Susan's father acknowledged the abuse in a conversation with her as she left, and he apologized for taking advantage of her all those years.

Susan experienced extreme bouts of depression, anger, and internal trauma as she embarked on a lengthy journey of recovery. While her father was the perpetrator, Susan was also hurt and confused about her relationship with her mother. It was not clear to Susan if her mother knew of the abuse when it was occurring or even after it happened. If she did know, Susan couldn't comprehend that her mother would be silent and wouldn't

PART 2—Forgiveness for Families

protect her. Susan wondered, if her mother didn't know, why not? Susan couldn't understand how her mother could have been oblivious to so many years of sexual abuse going on in their home. Her parents stayed married for their lifetime, and Susan's mother never acknowledged or denied to her the abuse that occurred.

At Susan's college, she was able to find a good counselor who provided many years of intense therapy and support. After graduating from college, Susan became successful in her career, married, and gave birth to a beautiful daughter. She continued to live in the same state as her parents, and when her daughter was five years old, her parents moved to the same town as Susan and her family. Susan maintained contact with her parents, but was very careful to never leave her daughter in her father's presence alone. Susan's parents had a swimming pool in their backyard, so the families would occasionally get together for swimming and barbecues.

The next summer, when her daughter was six, she received a telephone call from a police detective investigating a possible sexual assault by her father of a neighbor girl who had been swimming in her parent's pool. Susan felt like she had been punched in the stomach and a sick feeling crept through her entire body. Based on the description of the assault provided by the detective, Susan knew the girl was telling the truth because of the similarities to her own experience. The investigator said they wanted also to interview Susan's daughter and any other children who had been swimming in her parent's pool when her dad was present, in order to determine if others had also been sexually assaulted by him. Susan was convinced her daughter had not been abused by her father, since she made sure to always be present when her daughter was around, but she conceded to the interview to help the police.

Consumed with anger, Susan decided to confront her parents in their home. She showed up unannounced and demanded that her father confess to the police or she would tell the detective of his past history of abusing her. The confrontation was emotionally explosive and Susan fled as both her parents were moving towards her to physically attack.

Susan and her daughter showed up for their scheduled appointment with an investigator whose specialty was interviewing children. As her daughter was led into a play room for the interview, Susan assured her everything would be all right as Susan waited in the next room. After some time, the interviewer and Susan's daughter came out of the room and Susan noticed a stuffed animal clung tight in her daughter's arms. Susan knew

A Daughter Journeys from Incest to Healing

what this meant from her reading on the subject of child sexual abuse investigations. Stuffed animals are often used as a safe prop to help children tell what happened to them. Her daughter had been sexually assaulted in the pool by her own grandfather, Susan's father. Susan was now living her worst nightmare. As diligent as she had been, her daughter was still assaulted in the pool, even in her presence. Guilt consumed her initially for not knowing, and also for not reporting the abuse she had endured in her youth. Quickly however, Susan's entire attention shifted from her own pain to protecting her daughter and making sure it would never happen again.

Susan confided in the detective all of the sexual abuse she had experienced at the hands of her father. She had been abused in every way imaginable. Even though the statute of limitations had run out in her case, the prosecuting attorney submitted her testimony during the case and the judge took it into account when giving her dad a maximum prison sentence. He would spend his last years in prison. Susan had also taken the step of suing her parents for damages in civil court and was awarded a large financial settlement.

Many years later, when Susan's dad was still in prison, she decided to pursue victim-offender mediation and contacted a highly respected facilitator who was known for her humanistic approach to mediating such dialogue. Susan talked with the facilitator on the telephone at first, and then in person, many times over the course of a year to prepare to see her dad in prison. The facilitator helped Susan clarify her objectives for wanting to see her father and what she wanted to say to him. Susan's main objective was to peacefully hug him and say goodbye, since it would be the last time she would see him before his death. Additionally, she was hoping to fill in the gaps of memory that she had shut out during the abusive years, and she wanted to share good memories as well, since they had been close and had many positive experiences before the abuse occurred.

The facilitator, along with the prison social worker, also talked with Susan's father on many occasions to ensure his participation was consensual, without intent to do any harm to his daughter. The facilitator had concerns about bringing the two together, since it wasn't common for incest victims and offenders to pursue restorative dialogue due to the potential for re-victimization in what the perpetrator might say. Susan's father had refused treatment while in prison since he had virtually no chance of release before the end of his life, which was another concern of the facilitators. At this point Susan's father was in his seventies and in poor health. Last, when talking about his history of sexually abusing children, while he expressed deep regret and remorse for his abuse of Susan, he didn't acknowledge his abuse of his six-year-old granddaughter and the neighbor girl, and in fact put the blame on them.

Much of the preparation by the facilitator with Susan and her father individually focused on setting very clear boundaries about what they would talk about in this situation. Both still wanted to go ahead with the dialogue, but agreed to only discuss the history between Susan and her father, and not to discuss in any way the abuse of the two other girls. With this agreement, the facilitator felt she had the boundaries necessary to facilitate the conversation without threat of harm to Susan. If the conversation turned at any point, the facilitator was prepared to redirect or end the conversation.

The day of the mediation came. Susan met privately in the room with the facilitator first to review the dialogue process and facilitator's role, and then her father, the offender, was brought in to review the process again. The mediation lasted several hours. The facilitator asked Susan if she'd like to go first. Susan brought with her a small box of family photos to guide her sharing of the good times she remembered with her dad as a child. She talked about great times on fishing trips and family outings. She talked about traits of her dad's that she also shared and saw as positive in both of them. By talking about her good memories with her dad, Susan was able to say why and how it made it even harder to cope with the abuse, because they had been close and she had trusted him to keep her safe. Her dad listened and shared good memories as well. He expressed sincere and deep regret for having harmed her. Susan's father also expressed anger at Susan for suing him and her mother, to which Susan explained she needed her daughter to know that she did everything possible to stand up for her and protect her.

After both had said everything they wanted to say and the dialogue was coming to an end, Susan had one last thing she wanted to express to her dad. Susan said, "Dad, I'm probably never going to see you again, so I want you to know I love you," and she gave him a hug.

As a survivor of many years of incest, Susan's path of healing from the trauma brought her full circle to a restorative dialogue process with her father, the abuser. Even though the word *forgiveness* wasn't shared, as we continue to see in many powerful examples of the journey, the energy of forgiveness was present in Susan. It may be difficult to understand how the energy of forgiveness is found in situations of such deep victimization, yet what we see in Susan's case is that forgiveness does not mean ignoring the harm done, excusing it, or not expecting the perpetrator to be held accountable for his or her actions. All of these are still valid and important elements to repairing the harm. Yet, forgiveness comes from the heart and allows the victim to be freed from the burden carried internally when forgiveness isn't present.

PART 3
Forgiveness in Schools

CHAPTER 9
A Circle of Sixty Overcomes Racism

IN AN ATTEMPT TO address the education gap between white students and ethnic minority students in a Minneapolis suburban high school, the school district hired a consultant to explore innovative approaches to change the school climate. While African American and other ethnic minority students had lower graduation rates than their white counterparts, the problem was exacerbated by a disproportionate amount of violent incidents with and school suspensions of the minority students. Having learned of Oscar Reed's successful work with diverse youth in the metropolitan area, the consultant contacted him to bring his skills to the district.

That was the beginning of a long relationship between Oscar, an expert at facilitating circle dialogues with youth and developing their leadership to resolve conflicts among their peers, and the school district. For the past seven years, Oscar had been leading circle groups for high school students. After a few years of circles functioning well within the high school, the students encountered a conflict that required a process for resolution and healing.

Oscar established ethnic- and cultural-specific circles for students as a start, in order for them to connect with others with shared life experiences. Groups exist for male and female Latino, African American, and East African students, those groups with growing populations and most impacted by the education disparities in the district. Oscar notes, "While this may seem like a form of segregation, it's necessary to build their confidence, but as time moved on it opened up [to other ethnic groups]." The circles were held the same day each week but on alternating hours so students didn't miss the same class each week. This gave students a consistent structure to relate to each other, listen, and solve problems together. A set of principals supervised the circle process, with guidelines including listening without interruption when others are talking, no name-calling, and respecting the opinions of others while withholding judgment. A talking piece was passed around the circle, giving the person who held it the time to talk as others waited for their turns.

Once the groups were established, and the students had newfound confidence in their identity and ability, other students were welcomed to join and often invited by their peers already in the circle, or referred to the circles by other school staff. Each circle had three student co-captains as their leaders, adding to the sense of shared responsibility for the group.

The circle groups had been successfully established and supporting the leadership of youth for more than three years when the students noticed they weren't recognized as a student group or organization as other groups were within their school. One way this was evident was that other student groups were recognized and given credit in the school yearbook, but the circle groups had been left out. "The youth in the groups were really pissed off . . . seriously ready to riot they were so angry," Oscar recalled. It felt to them like an act of racism, since they were students of color not being recognized for their time commitment and leadership in their school environment. By this time, noticeable improvements had been made in the school environment, for which the students felt responsible. They were even being recognized by other school districts, frequently invited to give presentations about their way of running circles and the positive impact it had on the students, as well as the entire school. Structural racism is often hard to pinpoint, yet is still felt and experienced even if those who have the decision-making privilege are not aware of the impact of their actions. The students believed that racism was alive and well in their school, and something needed to change. They wanted those in charge to be held accountable for their actions.

Rather than rioting, however, the youth and Oscar decided to draw upon the experience they had gained in listening deeply and solving problems within the circle process, and invited the principal to join them for a circle dialogue. The students worked with Oscar to prepare how they would best handle the circle and give students a chance to participate. The principal accepted, and the circle was organized. Sixty youth came together for the circle, representing the various ethnic groups, with approximately thirty sitting in an inner circle with the principal and Oscar, and another thirty in an outer circle. A talking piece was held by the person whose turn it was to share thoughts and feelings, and it was passed around for each to take his or her turn, the principal being the last in the circle to speak.

The principal listened to each and every kid, with patience and no interruption. The students shared how they felt disregarded by their school due to their race and not being recognized for their contributions toward improving the school climate. They spoke responsibly and eloquently about their experiences and hopes for the future. After listening to the students, the principal spoke. He praised the youth for their efforts and apologized for what he perceived was an unintentional lack of recognition of their group. And to the surprise of everyone, he stopped the press on the printing of the yearbook.

"He literally stopped the press, in midstream of it being printed for that year, and made room for the circle groups to be included as a student organization in the current yearbook edition," Oscar shared. "I was just as surprised as the students. We thought the best outcome was that they would include the groups in the next yearbook, and didn't expect they would go to the expense of making the change in the current year, especially since the printing already began."

When Oscar talks about forgiveness as it relates to the student circles and their experience dealing with a circumstance perceived as structural racism, he attributes the students' participation in the process as a means for forgiveness becoming possible and changing the way in which people relate. Oscar emphasizes the importance of having guidelines for the circle dialogue, not rules, which changes the "way of being" in community. "Waiting to speak is a powerful thing," Oscar shares. By waiting to speak, people really listen to each other. The power of the circle is "all of these human beings are sitting together, experiencing life, and they come with experiences where they may need to hear from others to gain perspective. Then they don't feel so alone. The circle promotes a safe place, where you can expose yourself in a way that you usually don't do with a [school] social worker, for instance."

The principal, in speaking with Oscar, acknowledged that conflict and suspensions were down in the school by 40 percent and he asked Oscar if he knew why that was. Oscar looked at the principal waiting for his response, and the principal said, "It's because of the work you're doing with the students in circles."

Oscar was asked if forgiveness was present in the experience of the students in dealing with racism in their school. Oscar's response was,

"Absolutely. If I hear your story, I can now feel you and relate to where you're coming from. That's when forgiveness is possible. This may not be the case every time, but if you're living it, the way of being in the circle with others, hearing the stories, and feeling the compassion, it's possible. It takes practice."

Oscar and the students continue to share this experience in presentations to social work students and other groups years later, as an example of the transformation possible when they shifted their way of approaching a difficult situation that could have erupted into greater conflict. Their experience exudes the energy of forgiveness. It demonstrates how even the most difficult subjects, such as racism, can be addressed with compassion and understanding, which opens the door for positive changes beyond our expectations.

CHAPTER 10

A Classroom Out of Control Opens Up

ROBERT RICO WAS A police officer for twelve years when he decided to pursue a graduate degree in criminal justice. It was in graduate school that he was first exposed to the principals of restorative justice and he says, "It changed my life." He continued to work as a police officer for another eight years, but was increasingly frustrated as he didn't foresee any changes in the way the police force and community related to each other. He was compelled to change his career path in order to be a part of making things better. He says, "Love and forgiveness are needed in order to make changes," and Robert saw the principals of restorative justice as the path to bringing about positive changes in the way people solve problems together.

Robert was soon responsible for implementing a pilot program of restorative dialogue circles in an area school district. He shared this story on the power of the circle process with a sixth-grade class, and his reflection on forgiveness as it relates to the experience of everyone involved.

In his first year working with the school district, Robert partnered with other professionals to provide restorative justice training for teachers and school administrators. Several attended, and some were willing to work with the pilot program to bring restorative circle dialogue into their classrooms, while many were not yet open to the idea. Robert reflected, "It's amazing to me how we—police, teachers, administrators, and adults in general—silence kids. They have a lot to say, but we don't let them speak."

One sixth-grade teacher, who had attended the restorative justice pilot training, had an especially challenging classroom. The students were out of control, and the teacher had not been able to regain control of the classroom no matter what she tried. Mostly she saw this as stemming from one particular boy with whom she had regular confrontations. In utter frustration and looking for advice, she confided in Robert. After listening to her frustrations, Robert asked the teacher if she had tried a circle process in her classroom yet, and she said she hadn't, but since she had gone to the training she said she was willing to give it a try.

Robert checked in with other key stakeholders in the school to make sure they were on board with throom. He met with the vice principal and assistant teacher to hear their perspectives and ask for their participation in the circle, and both agreed. The students were likewise informed about the restorative circle dialogue process and also agreed it would be a good thing to try. A date was set for the first circle dialogue and the assistant principal agreed to facilitate.

The assistant principal came to the classroom with a talking piece and discussion questions he prepared in advance. He began with a review of the principles for how they would function together in the circle. The main thing was that whoever had the talking piece could speak from the heart, while others respectfully listened and waited patiently for their turn. As promised, the vice principal and assistant teacher participated in the circle, along with the teacher and fifteen sixth-grade students. The assistant principal offered the first question to which students could respond: "How are you doing in school?"

One by one, the students shared their feelings about how they were doing in school. When the talking piece reached the student who the teacher saw as being the most out of control and having a negative influence on the entire class, he first put his head down and didn't answer. The assistant principal encouraged him to take as much time as he needed; it was okay. Then, answering the question, the boy said quietly, "Not good. I'm not doing well at all. I'm having a hard time, and the last thing my dad told me was to do well in school."

He paused, as everyone listened in silence. Robert recalled, "The whole circle was just quiet, just listening." After all, this was the kid who was the tough guy, who caused problems for everyone and was out of control. He was even feared by other students. The boy spoke again, adding, "That's the last thing my dad said before he died." Robert looked over at the teacher, who at this point was crying. He looked at the boy who had also begun to cry, and other students were crying as well. "You could see a shift happening and it changed the relationship between the boy and the teacher. It's hard to explain the feeling in the room at that moment. They had never experienced this before. I could feel the emotional connection between the kid and the teacher. After this, their relationship improved. It was awesome," explained Robert.

After that, everyone wanted the talking piece. They all had something to say. They wanted to share their feelings in a deeper way with each other. One student said, "I want to do better, but I can't learn when everyone's acting up in class. I have a hard enough time as it is." Soon the students shifted the conversation to how they could help each other in the classroom; to improve their learning. All of the sixth graders were speaking freely. All were expressing their emotions. "I think they got to know each other better through the circle process. It was amazing," said Robert. The classroom environment continued to improve after the circle dialogue process began.

The experience of this sixth-grade classroom is representative of what we see on a regular basis in restorative dialogue circles. The shift in relationships can exceed our expectations and create space for group accountability and problem solving that may have been inconceivable previously. The word *forgiveness* was not raised in any of the preparation conversations or the circle dialogue, and yet the energy of forgiveness was present as students and the teacher shared on a deeper level. Relationships and the classroom environment changed for the better as a result.

PART 4

Forgiveness in Workplaces

CHAPTER 11

A Hospital Staff Transcends Workplace Tensions

INEVITABLY ANYONE WHO IS an employee in a workplace will experience some form of conflict, either directly or as an observer. Workplace conflict is often handled through avoidance, being ignored until someone leaves the work environment; or the conflict escalates until a supervisor removes one of the conflicting parties through job transfer or termination of their employment. In either case, the conflict is unresolved and bad feelings can linger. While it is still not a regular practice in most workplaces, many employers are beginning to see the benefits of restorative dialogue and the use of talking circles as a viable way to resolve conflicts and repair relationships, so that problems don't continue or escalate until out of control. Dr. Johnson's story is an example of a workplace conflict that was able to be addressed through a restorative dialogue process.

Dr. Johnson had been practicing medicine in a midwestern hospital for many years. He worked primarily in the emergency room. Over the past couple years of his tenure, a number of conflicts occurred around employment issues between Dr. Johnson and the hospital administration. None of the employment issues dealt with malpractice or the care received by patients, however tensions had increased between the doctor and other hospital staff, especially the administrators and nurses with whom Dr. Johnson most closely worked. The hospital administration decided to terminate his employment as a result.

Feeling the termination was unjustified and being angry about the way the situation was handled, Dr. Johnson decided to consult an attorney. After listening to Dr. Johnson's account of what had happened at the hospital, his attorney advised him that he would have a good chance of winning in a court of law. With that, Dr. Johnson chose to undertake litigation. The case took many months in court with the review of hospital personnel records and depositions, but ultimately the judge ruled on the side of Dr. Johnson. The outcome was the reinstatement of Dr. Johnson's previous position in the hospital.

Hospital administrators and staff were surprised when they heard the decision of the court and immediately started feeling stressed that the doctor would be returning to their hospital. Some of them had offered written testimony of previous conflict with Dr. Johnson and the last thing they wanted was for things to go back as they were. They worried that tensions would be even worse following months of legal action. Administrators had similar worries, since they had terminated Dr. Johnson with no consideration that he might return. Administrators also wanted to make sure staff morale wasn't diminished.

The hospital was progressive in its practices and policies to handle employee conflict, which would become very important in the reinstatement of Dr. Johnson. Hospital personnel policies offered all employees personal coaching from a trained professional in handling conflict in the workplace. Mediation was also offered as an option to handle conflict among employees as well as between employees and their supervisors. If both parties agreed, a confidential mediator would be provided to assist with conflict resolution at no charge to the employees. Given the scope of Dr. Johnson's history with the hospital, the administrators, and numerous staff, the administrators decided more than mediation would be necessary to reintegrate Dr. Johnson into the workplace. They contacted the hospital's professional mediation consultant to find the best option, and were referred to Janine Geske, a retired judge whose expertise is restorative justice mediation and who is experienced with using the circle dialogue process to restore relationships in serious group conflict situations.

Janine agreed to meet with two hospital administrators to review the situation. Since Dr. Johnson would certainly be returning to the hospital, the main intent of the administrators in holding a circle dialogue with employees was to give everyone a safe space to get reacquainted and share their hopes and concerns moving forward, so morale wouldn't be affected. They definitely didn't want to repeat past conflicts, and were looking to Janine to guide the conversation in a way that promoted healing from past conflict while setting expectations for the future. Janine agreed to lead a half-day circle dialogue with twelve employees, including Dr. Johnson, administrators, nurses, and other frontline hospital staff.

To prepare, Janine had telephone conversations with each of the staff invited to join in the half-day dialogue. Each agreed to participate, as did Dr. Johnson. Some people said they had no problem with Dr. Johnson before he was let go from his position, but were concerned about how relationships would be in the workplace after a major legal battle that forced the hospital to take him back. Others who were more directly involved had some hard feelings towards Dr. Johnson from past work conflict and wanted to clear the air before working with him again. Some expressed "not getting along" with Dr. Johnson in the past. They didn't want to dread going to work every day. In spite of some apprehension, all were looking for the process to, at a minimum, reestablish relationships so their work environment would be cordial and patient care wouldn't suffer.

The half-day gathering was held at a neutral location in a comfortable room set up with snacks and beverages. Chairs were formed in the shape of a circle. In preparation, Janine carefully and thoughtfully developed questions that would allow for safe sharing among participants. As hospital staff, administrators, and Dr. Johnson arrived, they were welcomed by Janine and encouraged to sit where they felt most comfortable in the circle.

Janine began the circle by reviewing the process and a set of guidelines for everyone to follow. The first questions asked by Janine were to help surface what people had in common as a safe basis for their future work relationships. One by one the hospital staff and Dr. Johnson shared why they chose a career in medicine, followed by each sharing a touching experience they had while working in the hospital. Janine, seeing a level of comfort and safety forming among those in the circle, probed into the more difficult areas. She asked people to share the problem areas of the past and how they wanted the environment to be different in the future. She asked them to talk about any "elephants in the room," to make sure no issue went unmentioned. Last, they talked about how they wanted to work together and what each of them could do to make that happen moving forward.

Step by step throughout their time together, barriers from their past experiences were broken and the hospital personnel were ready to move forward in their work relationships. Reflecting on the experience, Janine commented, "The time together in circle was truly transformational for the hospital staff and Dr. Johnson. They had such great relief from not having to deal with each other for the first time in the emergency room. Of course this was the beginning and a lot more was still to be done, but they all wanted to be a part of making it better moving forward."

In this hospital situation where conflict escalated to the termination of a doctor followed by major litigation and then return of the doctor to the workplace by court order, forgiveness was in question at many levels. The circle process facilitator who helped them move forward says the word *forgiveness* was never raised, but an intentional release of past conflict occurred in the group, shifting the energy among people. The energy of forgiveness was present as people opened up to the possibility of rebuilding trust. Colleagues transformed the situation and reestablished relationships with new expectations for working together. This doesn't mean they had forgotten about their past experiences, but it does mean they chose to learn from those experiences and have agreed to take responsibility as a group for moving forward in a different way.

CHAPTER 12

A Nonprofit Agency Finds a New Beginning

JAMES WAS PURSUING A graduate degree, during which time he was in a service learning position with a nonprofit organization working with youth. Major changes happened at that time, sending the organization into a tailspin. After finishing his education, James returned to the organization as a consultant and found himself in the middle of deep-rooted workplace conflicts that were potentially lethal for the organization. The way James handled the situation exemplifies the energy of forgiveness as it plays out in a work setting.

The nonprofit social service organization had been started forty-three years ago by a strong African American mother and her daughter. The mother, Rosemary, was a civil rights activist in Milwaukee and was very well known. Her daughter, Chanda, was also well known, with a reputation of being a mover and shaker who could get things done on behalf of the African American community.

These two women built the organization and maintained it for most of its life. They were in the picture in a big way. Rosemary died at 103 years of age, and Chanda died a few years later, still holding the position of chief executive officer in the organization. Not only did the organization lose its leader, Chanda had actually passed away in her office, so the trauma for the organization and staff was intensified. To keep the legacy going, Chanda's son Roland took over the leadership of the organization. His intention was to run the organization as his mother had, upholding his grandmother's and mother's great work. In reality, Roland was in mourning when he made this decision. Everyone in the organization was also still in mourning. Even though Roland had good intentions, he was not his mother. His mother had set the bar very high. There was a lot going on. James first came into the organization to work on a specific project for a short period, but felt compelled to return to assist after finishing his law degree.

The staff and Roland struggled to move forward but they were not very successful at it, and the staff had the lowest morale ever. Roland was trying to fill his mother's shoes and do things his mother's way, but he wasn't his mother and couldn't pull it off. It was an all-time low for the organization. They had lost a lot of funding—about two million in just four years. The budget was way off balance. The board of directors was unhappy with the chief executive officer, the chief executive officer was unhappy with the board, and the staff was unhappy with the board and the chief executive officer. The organization's atmosphere was very contentious and chaotic. People involved had a lot of things they needed to say to each other, but weren't. Instead, side conversations and resentful actions were hurting a lot of people.

James knew that for the organization to move forward and survive, a great deal of healing needed to take place. Because of his exposure to restorative justice, James felt a restorative dialogue process was the best way to go in order to begin the healing journey.

As a part of his work, James organized and facilitated a circle discussion between a representation of board members, staff, and key community stakeholders. The leadership of the board participated in the circle, as well as any staff who wanted to participate. For the most part it was staff that had been there for a very long time that chose to participate. Some had been there as long as thirty to forty years, so the feelings ran deep. "For the old timers, they were literally stuck in the past," added James. James took the time to talk with everyone in advance of the circle dialogue, so they were fully prepared for the circle process.

When the circle began, James led with a set of questions he had developed to ensure everyone felt safe, and so the topic would stay relevant as they moved on. An important development in the circle dialogue occurred when the talking piece reached Roland and it was his turn to share. He admitted to the group how difficult the leadership position had been for him. He didn't expect it to be so challenging. His intent was to uphold his mom's legacy, but he felt like he was failing. Roland shed some tears during the circle, which demonstrated his willingness to be vulnerable, while also showing his sincerity in his commitment to the organization and intent to carry on the legacy. The staff in the circle surprisingly shared that they hadn't really given Roland a chance. They had a hard time letting go of

Chanda after her being the leader for decades. James noted, "I think the best thing that came out of the circle was that the chief executive officer and the board let their guards down and were honest with each other." The board members saw the strong commitment of the staff and chief executive officer, and recommitted to the mission and vision of the organization.

Shortly after the circle process, about four members of the board retired. Roland as well decided it was time for him to step down. "It was the time for change and it happened in a good way," said James. Everyone left without animosity towards each other or the organization. Previously, some staff who wanted to be the chief executive officer felt overlooked, which had increased the resentment towards Roland. When Roland saw it was in his and the organization's interest for him to move on, it also gave others a chance to vie for the position. This decreased past animosity.

The board and James decided to have a strategic planning retreat as a next step in the process. They gave staff a more active role in the organization in order for them to feel they could have a voice in decision-making. They established committees, like a staff development committee, and also a visions committee (charged with going through every program and doing evaluation and planning). People thought the organization had lost focus, so the goal was to connect the programs back to the mission and pursue funding that aligned with the mission. James served as interim director for nine months to help the organization through this time. He assisted the organization in recruiting a permanent chief executive officer and then stepped down as interim.

When asked about the role of forgiveness in resolving the deep-rooted workplace conflict, James said the actual word *forgiveness* wasn't used. However, other phrases like, "I understand," "I know how you feel," "I'm sorry that happened," and "I can't imagine what that was like for you," were all used and were an important part of the process. James emphasized, "Most often, 'I understand' was repeated and very important in the process. It felt like forgiveness was happening among people."

PART 5

Forgiveness for Communities

CHAPTER 13

An Act of Vandalism Engages a High School

WHEN HALF A DOZEN high school students decided to "trash" the yard of another student from their school, they certainly thought that it was all "fun and games." And even when the case entered a restorative justice process in collaboration with school administrators and local law enforcement, the students continued to think to themselves, "What's the big deal? We meant no harm." But little did they know how much harm had truly rippled out from the epicenter of their actions. Not only was one family deeply impacted, but a larger community of people experienced a tense atmosphere of imbalance that needed restoration. In the end, these students went from feeling little empathy and minimizing their actions to feeling genuine remorse and taking responsibility for their actions. That shift made all the difference.

One way to better understand how negative emotional energies can build up between offending parties and victimized parties is to observe the friction caused by minimizing tendencies on the part of offenders and the need for validation on the part of victims. Like two hands rubbing against each other to create heat, these two responses also move in opposite directions; as they continue to rub against each other in strong, "pressing" ways, they are bound to build up a store of negatively charged energies. It is important to recognize too that from the victim's point of view, the experience of this mounting tension is a secondary impact upon their lives, following the primary impact caused by the offense itself. Effective restorative justice responses will help to address both layers of impact for victims, and simultaneously help offenders take responsibility on both levels: making amends for damages, but also taking ownership for what they did along with its lingering effects. Both external and internal dimensions need to be addressed for full resolution.

The clearest expression of this negative energy at work occurred in the final resolution meeting when thirty people, with two facilitators from a community-based restorative justice program, met to bring dialogue and closure. It was a two-hour meeting, and even three-quarters of the way through the meeting, most of the participants, especially the facilitators, could tell that things were not reaching a satisfying end. But fortunately there was a breakthrough that was triggered from an unexpected voice within the group, and everything shifted. More on that to come.

As the two facilitators had previously met with both the offending and victimized parties separately, they learned the details of the initial offense as well as the background to some escalating tensions. The half-dozen students, both male and female, all seniors and all within the more popular circles of the school, had decided to turn up the rival tensions between their class and the junior class. A history of rivalry had already been in play, and so when these students secretly conspired to vandalize and disarray the front yard of another girl's home, it seemed to be a normal, fun thing for high school kids to do. Julie Stenson, the student whose home became the target, was seen as a prime representative of the other class. Several factors, however, complicated the choice of this particular home. Julie's father worked at the school, and her mother was very much involved in the work world of the local town.

This foray in the night went far beyond the toilet-papering of tree branches. It involved some egging, some car soaping, but it also went into the realm of hurtful symbolic messaging. These communications included the writing of profanity, the display of some sexual paraphernalia, and the smearing of feces. Needless to say, when members of the Stenson family awoke the next morning, they were stunned and shocked. It took amazing strength on their part to even clean up the litter and displays, not only because they had to emotionally engage the message and intent of the vandalism, but also because they had to bear the embarrassment of having neighbors view it all and possibly wonder the worst. Questions filled the thoughts of Julie and her family, weighing down their hearts. "Who would do such a thing? And why did they do it? And why did they do it to us?" In the following days, the Stensons were thankful to have some neighbors come to their support and express a sense of "we're in this difficult experience with you."

An Act of Vandalism Engages a High School

Imagine, though, what it was like for Julie and Mr. Stenson to come to school that day, let alone the next several days, before the offenders were clearly identified. And once the six students were identified, imagine what it was like for the Stensons to be in proximity to these students without having most of their questions answered. Imagine too how fast the word spread throughout the community, impacting Mrs. Stenson's world. This emotional roller coaster experience on the part of the Stensons provides a window into seeing how the negative energy stemming from the offense itself was compounded when the family indirectly heard and felt that the offenders were on a pathway of minimizing the whole affair.

As the incident happened off school property, the case normally would have been processed by the city police. But since the roots of the alleged rivalry were in the school community, and the ongoing impacts of the incident created a tense imbalance within the school community, the principal chose to invite the local restorative justice program to oversee the process. No charges were filed. Community service and other consequences had already been set in place, but it was clear that a community-level dialogue process was necessary to bring the whole matter to a better end. The two facilitators then scheduled two preparation meetings with each party. After both meetings with the students who did the vandalizing, the facilitators debriefed each other about how there was very little empathy being expressed, and how the main sentiment was summed up as, "Why make a mountain out of a molehill?" Nevertheless, all parties voluntarily agreed to attend a large restorative conference meeting that would meet in the school cafeteria one evening.

A double circle process was used to help this conference distinguish those who would do the talking (the inner circle), and those who were there to listen, give support, and bear witness (the outer circle). Along with the six offenders in the inner circle, the Stensons were joined by supporters, another couple from their neighborhood. In the outer circle were mostly parents of the offenders and some school staff, including the principal. The facilitators invited all in the inner circle to share their stories and to respond to what they heard. This all took some time, and after about one-and-a-half hours, one facilitator noted to the group that the offending students were using a lot of "we" language. Some apologies were made, but they didn't go very deep. An ambiguous tension was still in the air, and the general mood was, "I wish this all could just be over."

At a critical moment, the husband of the support couple to the Stensons spoke his mind freely. He said in effect, "Look, none of us are going to leave here this evening feeling very good unless each of you [meaning the six students] start to talk honestly from the heart about what you alone did that night. It's time you start saying, 'I did this . . . ,' and then apologize to the Stensons." An awkward silence followed and the facilitators allowed the silence to remain. Then one girl, the one student who relative to the others had previously expressed more concern and empathy, broke the ice and said, "I was the one who did . . .". And when she ended with her apology, it struck everyone deeply in a profound, positive way. The logjam of negative energy was dislodging, and everyone could feel the shift. One by one, each of the other five students used "I" language for what they did, adding a new apology from the heart. Throughout this segment, Kleenex boxes were constantly in motion in both inner and outer circles.

Not much more needed to be said. A couple of practical agreements were determined for making further amends, but in light of the huge relief that everyone felt in the room, it seemed as if deep resolution had come out of the dialogue. All the negative emotions were released and a new peace was born within that group. The Stensons communicated to all that they were thankful for what finally happened in the meeting, and the facilitators brought the conference to a close. The most telling display of resolution actually came after people got up from their seats. No one left the cafeteria for another full thirty minutes. Adults had opportunity to connect with other adults, free now to have conversations that were no longer strained or limited. Julie must have been hugged by all of the other students, and there was no desire on their part to leave the scene.

In a very real sense, the negative energy (built up from both the offense and the lack of genuine ownership and empathy) found an avenue to be transformed into the positive energy of forgiveness. Such forgiveness is synonymous with the term "release." As pent-up emotions can have great influence on communities that don't allow for deep understanding and breakthrough, it is clear that good resolution processes need to help people deal with the flow of emotional energy in constructive ways. In that aftermath time of informal mingling, a police officer who was in the outer circle came up to one of the facilitators. The facilitator, from previous conversations, knew that this officer carried a natural skepticism for any restorative process that seemed "touchy-feely." But his comment shows how powerful a restorative process can be to help the whole community. In three short words he said, "This was good."

CHAPTER 14
A Neo–Nazi Youth Offers to Apologize

Rabbi Benjamin arrived at his office Friday morning a few minutes after nine. He felt a cool winter breeze and within minutes found the entire front window of the temple shattered, with several bullet holes in the interior wall.

"Thank God no one was in the building at the time of this shooting."

An increasing sense of vulnerability, fear, and anger pulsated through every fiber of his being. It was as though the entire weight of the historical trauma of the Jewish people rested on his shoulders. Yes, there had been previous incidents of anti-Semitism in this small midwestern community, but nothing of this magnitude had ever occurred.

Rabbi Benjamin immediately called the police and then other leaders in the congregation. After extensive investigation, the police determined that this act of vandalism, a hate crime, was likely perpetrated by a local cell of young neo-Nazis that they had been watching.

Within ten days, the police had arrested and charged three young men, two of whom had extensive prior arrests related to hate crimes. These two secured a well-known defense attorney and pled not guilty, hoping to avoid conviction, since they believed the prosecutors had only circumstantial evidence; however, both were eventually convicted and sentenced to prison.

The third young man arrested was seventeen. It was Alex's first trouble with the law. The prosecutors consulted with Rabbi Benjamin and referred the young man to a local restorative justice program that would allow interested members of the congregation to meet him, express their anger, talk about the historical trauma of the Jewish people, and get answers to many questions. Most did not want to meet this young neo-Nazi. For many, to even walk into the same room and talk with this "monster" was to recognize

PART 5—Forgiveness for Communities

his humanity. It disrespected the painful legacy of their people. Some had family members who were killed in the gas chambers of the Nazi regime in Germany during the past century.

Ultimately, Rabbi Benjamin and twenty-three other members of the congregation agreed to meet Alex. Who was he? How could he commit such a terroristic hate crime? What about his parents? Did he know anything at all about the history and trauma of the Jewish people? This meeting would only happen if all, including this young neo-Nazi, were willing. It was voluntary. After much thought and in recognition that a far more harsh punishment could await him, Alex agreed to meet Rabbi Benjamin and the others.

A mediator from the local restorative justice program met with the congregation's members to help prepare them for this meeting with Alex. He then met with Alex a week later to prepare him for the meeting. All involved were very anxious about the eventual meeting, not knowing what to expect. The mediator, Rick, met several more times with the two sides over the next two weeks. Finally, they seemed ready and willing to proceed.

The meeting was convened in a conference room at a local community center. Chairs were set in a large circle. Rabbi Benjamin and the members of the congregation arrived first and were seated. Ten minutes later Alex entered the room with the mediator's assistant. The tension and anxiety in the room were palpable.

The energy of both anger and vulnerability was intense. Rick opened the meeting with a moment of silence. He then offered a few brief comments, explaining how the circle process works. Rick would ask a series of questions, beginning with introductions, and a talking stick would be passed clockwise around the circle. Only the person who received the talking stick was to have the opportunity to speak or pass it on if they had nothing to say. All others were to listen to the person with the talking stick, without comments or questions.

Later on, the talking stick would be put aside and cross talk could occur, with specific questions asked and answered. Any plan to repair the harm caused by Alex would need to be agreed upon by all. It would then be written and presented to the prosecutors as a plan to hold Alex accountable. If successfully completed, Alex would avoid a prison sentence, although several weekends in the local jail might be required based on the recommendations of all those present in the circle.

A Neo–Nazi Youth Offers to Apologize

The talking stick was passed to Rabbi Benjamin, who sat to the left of Rick. The rabbi held the piece in silence, in deep reflection. After several minutes, he began to speak of the hatred and terror the Jewish people have experienced throughout history. Rabbi Benjamin went into specific details about the death of his mother in the gas chambers of the Nazis during the Holocaust and the impact of this trauma on his life. Fifteen minutes later he passed the talking stick to the next person. Other members of the congregation expressed similar themes, including anger at the horror of such a hate crime.

When the talking stick finally came to Alex he was visibly nervous and unable to look directly at others. After several minutes he began to speak of his difficulty in fully understanding the impact of what he did until this meeting. Alex's parents and uncle taught him from birth about white power and the honor of protecting his race from Jews and blacks. Until now Alex actually thought that what he had done was honorable.

This was extremely hard for the rabbi and the others to hear, but they listened. Alex began to slowly express the emotional energy of shame for his behavior, though not yet the much-desired words of apology. When he was finished, the talking stick again went around the circle. The comments now offered by Rabbi Benjamin and many, but not all, of the congregational members present had a different energy. Voice tones were more subdued, even difficult to hear at times. The most vocally angry and loud participant before Alex spoke now offered comments that many would find hard to believe.

"Before, I thought you were a monster. Having heard your story I now see a frightened young kid who was acting out his truth, the misguided truth of your parents. You haven't said the words, but I feel you expressing a genuine sense of shame for your behavior."

Rick was gently nodding as this comment was offered. Seven more members of the synagogue made comments about what they were experiencing, witnessing a scared young kid facing the real human impact of his actions.

Rick invited comments about developing a plan to repair the harm caused by Alex, to the extent this was realistically possible. Rabbi Benjamin stated that the cost of repairing the window and wall with the bullet holes must be the starting point. All nodded, including Alex. Many other ideas were presented for repairing the harm. Finally all agreed that in addition to financial restitution for repairing the damage, Alex would attend three lectures on the history and beliefs of Judaism, as well as attend two Friday

PART 5—Forgiveness for Communities

evening services at the synagogue, to be followed by a meal with the rabbi and other interested persons.

Alex nervously agreed to this plan while also thinking it might have been easier to just spend time in jail watching TV. The prosecutors accepted this plan. Upon completing these responsibilities over the next six months, Alex was invited into the home of the rabbi, along with several of the most initially angry participants. They shared a meal together and reflected on what all had experienced in this restorative justice circle process. Rabbi Benjamin and several others now consider Alex to be part of their family, an outcome no one could ever have anticipated.

All who participated in this process danced with the energy of severe conflict and trauma, sometimes expressing their strong views and sometimes listening. Words were necessary and helpful, but oftentimes lacking. Yet the emotional presence and vulnerability of all involved parties led to transformation and healing, to a renewed sense of compassion, connection, and reconciliation. Without the words being expressed, the energy of forgiveness was palpable.

CHAPTER 15

A 9/11 Death Threat Opens a Door for Muslims

A FEW HOURS AFTER watching live footage of the September 11 terrorist attacks on TV, Christopher Younce, a thirty-three-year-old man from Eugene, Oregon, went to his phone book, looked up the Islamic Cultural Center in his area, and made a call. Tammam Adi, who is a prominent leader of the local Muslim community, answered the phone. The person on the other end raged and spewed profanities.

Adi tried calming the man, telling him, "Maybe we should wait to see who really did it." Christopher Younce didn't want to listen or reason and continued his tirade, even threatening death to all Muslims. Tammam Adi hung up, but Younce called back and this time left a very incriminating message on the answering machine.

Adi was frozen with fear and uncertainty. His and his wife's fears of retaliation were palpable. In the Middle East, where Mr. Adi came from, death threats are taken very seriously. The two were left feeling "like sitting ducks," and immediately contacted the Human Rights Commission to enlist help and protection. The group was able to trace the call and identify the caller. Younce was arrested, and released after a short time.

Soon after the district attorney's office noted the offender lived in the Bethel neighborhood, which meant that instead of going to court, Younce could go in front of a new Community Accountability Board that was part of a local restorative justice initiative. The assistant to the DA was a strong restorative justice advocate and had worked with the Community Accountability Board on previous cases. She referred the case to the Restorative Justice Program of Community Mediation Services.

PART 5—Forgiveness for Communities

Two other important factors helped bring the case to a restorative justice meeting. First, the once-belligerent caller told the prosecuting attorney of his intent to apologize and make amends. And second, the Muslim leader and his wife expressed willingness to speak with the man who had threatened them. If the restorative justice conference was unsuccessful, the district attorney's office made it clear to the Adis that they would continue with full prosecution.

The facilitator of this conference, Ted Lewis, held several separate meetings with Younce and the Adis. During these meetings, Lewis and two other co-mediators listened to how this event affected the Adis and Younce, learned of their needs, and introduced them to how the eventual face-to-face meeting in the presence of other concerned community members would unfold. Younce indicated during the preparation meetings that he had acted out of rage, yelling into the phone, wanting to blame and to scare the Muslim leader.

Younce said he had equated all Arab Muslims with terrorist extremists like Osama Bin Laden. Now, he felt badly about what he had done and was ashamed of the publicity. The Associated Press headline on September 13 read, "Eugene man charged with threatening Muslims."

Younce had a long history of anger problems, which reached crisis levels after the death of his son and a recent job loss. Although he had felt the need for counseling, he never took that step. Just hours prior to meeting with mediators, however, he finally called a therapist. Opening the phone book to find the number, he turned to the same page where he had found the number for the mosque. He had a jolt of insight. "I went to the very page looking for help that I went to in order to create the problem," he said.

Younce learned about restorative justice and its focus on repairing the harm done to specific victims. He wanted to apologize in person to the Muslim leader and his family, and do whatever was asked of him to make things right. He wanted the opportunity to show them that he was a better man than his actions suggested. "I'd like a peaceful solution," Younce said.

When Lewis and the other two mediators met with the Adis, a husband and wife who ran the Islamic Center, and the director of the local Human Rights Commission, two points emerged. First, the couple had been traumatically affected by the hate call, and second, they were committed to finding some way of mending the harm. After responding sensitively to the first concern, listening respectfully to the victims' experiences of harm, the

A 9/11 Death Threat Opens a Door for Muslims

mediators were able to address the couple's second concern, building trust in the potential for a peaceful resolution.

At the heart of the husband's concern was motive. "Why did he do it to us?" Mr. Adi was a scientist, and needed to account for the causes behind actions. He wanted to meet with the offender and hear him say why he did it and, hopefully, why he wouldn't do it again.

A police officer was assigned to protect the Adi family; he would open their mail, check their car, and accompany them to speaking engagements. Mrs. Adi, like many Muslim women fearing retaliation, stopped wearing the hijab, the traditional scarf Muslim women wear around their head and neck. A boy approached their daughter at her high school and said, "We should round up all the Muslims and shoot them." A simple phone call would rattle them, as it could be another threat. Throughout this intake meeting, the victims repeatedly turned the conversation to the topic of negative stereotypes fostered by popular media.

The first joint meeting between victims and offender was set for nearly one month after the tragedy. Several members of the Community Accountability Board, along with the prosecuting attorney, the assigned police officer, the mediators, a representative from the Human Rights Commission, and support parties for both victim and offender were in attendance. Lewis served as lead facilitator.

There was a lot of emotional tension in the room. Lewis acknowledged the unique aspects of this case in light of the September 11 attacks. Noting that harm was caused by destructive words, he highlighted the importance of using constructive words in this restorative justice process.

Younce apologized early on, but the Adis doubted his sincerity. Younce had to convince the Adis and the Community Board that he meant what he said. If he didn't, the prosecuting attorney was prepared to file criminal charges against him.

The community members had important things to say to both parties. They made several empathetic statements to the Adis and conveyed to Younce that they were there to support his process of accountability and reintegration into his community. Younce, though appreciative of the process, was overwhelmed by all of their questions. The pressure to say the right thing was almost too much.

Tammam Adi was not able to make eye contact with the offender, though his wife was able. Mr. Adi acknowledged this was so; he had come into this joint meeting feeling more fearful, more vulnerable than ever. Due to the fear on both Mr. Adi's and Christopher Younce's parts, not much more progress was made.

In spite of the limited success of the first meeting, everyone agreed to meet again in order to work toward a better sense of resolution. During the following weeks, Lewis checked in with the parties by phone, and was encouraged to learn that everyone was still invested in the process. The Adis needed to spend more time going over the questions they wanted answered, and firming up their requests for restitution. They were still struggling with questions like, "Did he act alone or as a member of a racist group? Was this a first-time racist act, or part of an ongoing pattern? What was in his mind between the time of seeing the news and picking up the phone?"

The Adis needed to hear Younce state why he did it, and why he wouldn't do it again. They also wanted very much to know whether negative stereotypes in the news media played a role in the offense. They were trying to figure out for themselves why they were under attack.

When the parties came together for the second meeting, the initiating process was the same as it was the first time, but this time a court reporter from the region's primary newspaper came to this meeting, which was part of the effort to engage the public on the danger of negative stereotypes of Muslims. Lewis explained that the reporter was there "off the record," but would likely be involved in follow-up interviews and future coverage.

Younce provided an update on his progress with counseling, with his family and relatives, and with his job. He mentioned that he had told his employer about the whole situation, which impressed the victims. Most importantly, he brought up the death of his infant son, helping the Adis understand the very real, human suffering behind Younce's misdirected rage.

Tammam Adi responded, addressing a string of questions to the offender. Younce did his best to answer, covering much of the same ground he had covered in the first meeting. Only this time, Mr. Adi was better able to take in the answers offered. "I'm satisfied with what I have heard," he said in response. "I think we can move forward."

With this, a profound shift of energy took place in the room. The prevailing tensions were exchanged for a lighter, more optimistic mood. After a short break, the group began to discuss options for restitution. The Adis asked for a public letter of apology to the Muslim community. They also wanted Younce to attend two upcoming lectures on the religion of Islam. After further discussion three more agreements were added: Younce would cooperate in news coverage of the case, commit to continue his counseling,

A 9/11 Death Threat Opens a Door for Muslims

and speak to teens in juvenile detention about his experience. The assistant district attorney created a written document that was signed by all parties.

At one point the concern was raised that Younce's new job might be jeopardized by the media coverage. Mr. Adi offered to personally talk to the employer in order to help the offender keep his job. Younce was moved by this, but acknowledged he was willing to accept any and all consequences for his actions.

At the close of the meeting, Tammam Adi unexpectedly reached across the table to shake Younce's hand. It was a moving gesture that spoke eloquently of the progress the two parties had made. Once the agreement was signed, those present got up and began shaking hands with one another in good spirits, buoyed by the sense of relief and reconciliation in the room.

In the end, Christopher Younce did comply with all terms in the restitution agreement, even sitting next to Tammam's wife at one of the Islamic lectures. He later spoke to Lewis by phone saying that he had enjoyed being there, had learned a lot, and was motivated to attend additional lectures on his own.

A number of factors contributed to a successful resolution of this conflict, including a remorseful offender and a victim committed to peaceful dialogue. The community had an established restorative justice program, and collaboration between the agencies providing services to both victim and offender. Finally, all involved were committed to working through the tense emotions toward eventual resolution. Their story and others like it show how community reconciliation and personal growth can emerge from some of our most painful life experiences. The words and thoughts of forgiveness never arose during the lengthy preparation and the eventual face-to-face dialogue. Yet the shift in energy from anger and hostility to understanding and compassion was truly palpable. This encounter changed and enriched their lives.

Note: Real names and actual events are described in this very public story that has appeared in several newspaper articles.

CHAPTER 16

A Community Circle Changes Everyone's Hearts

ONE OF THE BIGGEST challenges for offenders who come from urban environments is to regain the trust of the communities to which they return. It may seem that it is all up to them to make the best of it, to find a job, and to turn away from a life of crime. But a deeper look may well show that the community also bears a responsibility to make an offender's reintegration successful. Certainly if communities can shut the door on a returning offender, refusing employment, for instance, they can also open that door.

A restorative justice circle program in a south side neighborhood of Milwaukee took these matters to heart. Most restorative programs work off the triangle model of giving equal attention to victims, offenders, and the community. But sometimes the community can get the short end of the stick. The Milwaukee program, however, gave the community a heightened role in their processes, recognizing that the community needs to be served well but it can also be serving well. Over time, it was discovered that the numerous community members from the neighborhood who sat in circle processes with offenders and victims had their hearts changed as much as any of the most serious offenders present.

Participating now and then in these weekly reentry or reintegration circles was former Wisconsin Supreme Court judge Janine Geske. She was able to narrate the many benefits of these dialogue experiences, highlighting the role of the community. Sometimes acting as a circle keeper (the one who sets the tone, explains the talking piece, and initiates the questions), Janine came to open circles with a question that put everyone on equal footing: "What is the impact of violence on your life?" She recognized that this is not only a question for victims alone, but an important question for

A Community Circle Changes Everyone's Hearts

offenders as well. Most offenders bear long histories of being victimized in earlier years. Having them talk about their own stories of past hurt was a way to make them feel more human and more connected to everyone else. It was an important way of equalizing everyone who sat in the circle. Janine also understood that people representing the community have something to say about how they, as community members, have had their lives affected by violence. This speaks to how the effects of violence can ripple outward and touch all parts of a community for the worse.

In the Milwaukee program, it was routine to invite police officers to take part in these circles. This inclusion became an important way to build stronger community relations between offenders and officers, which otherwise could remain strained for decades. One time, as people in the circle began to open up with their stories of past pain, an officer shared about a time he was the first to show up at a shooting scene, only to enter a living room with a little girl who had been tragically shot in the head. He described how he held her close to him, and in a short time, she breathed her last breath in his arms. He was never able to get this little girl out of his head. He told the group that every time he is assigned to a shooting scenario, he "carries" her with him in his mind. For ex-offenders in the circle to listen to such a story is a way to truly build new bridgework between the police and offenders.

Janine also participated in a circle where an African American man, Morris, imprisoned several times for armed robbery and other crimes, spoke openly about his efforts of reintegration after leaving prison. Morris explained how each time he got out, folks in the community would just say, "Go get a job!" Morris certainly wanted to get a job, but every time he tried to apply, he had doors, figuratively speaking, slammed in his face. He then told the group, "Now that I'm out the third time, I will try again, because I really do want to work. But if the same thing happens again, and doors are slammed in my face, I'm going to return to crime. I don't have any other choice." Morris also went on to share about the hardships of his boyhood. He spoke about times when he had been abused and neglected, and how all of this had set the stage for an unstable life that led to crime in the first place.

It so happened that in the circle was a white police officer who had been deeply moved by what Morris had been saying, and took his words to heart. This officer was a community liaison officer who knew the neighborhood well, and knew all of the "troublemakers" in the area. But something shifted in his mind as he heard Morris open up about his past and about his

PART 5—Forgiveness for Communities

challenges in finding a job. After the formal circle dialogue was over, this officer went up to him and said, "For the first time, I understand how you got to where you got. I am not giving you a pass on the bad choices you've made. But if you are really serious about getting a job, I will help you."

They chatted a bit, and the officer wished Morris luck, and gave him his calling card. Later, Morris said to the circle keeper, "I've never had a police officer talk to me like that." Both Morris and the officer entered a new zone of listening and communication that had never been available to them before.

Not long after this circle meeting, following several job searching efforts, Morris went to the district police station and looked up the officer. The two of them reconnected, and Morris said he had been trying to find good employment, and that he had a child who needed health insurance. The officer then said he would help, but in light of all his past experiences with young men, he wanted to test Morris's commitment. "If you show up here at the station at 8:30 every morning for two weeks, just as you would for a normal job, then I will know that you are truly serious. Are you willing to do that?" Morris said yes without hesitation. The two weeks passed, and Morris fulfilled his commitment. The officer then contacted a prosecutor who was a friend of his, and together with Morris, went to a job site where Morris could apply for a job. The manager expressed some hesitations, recounting how things with the last felon he hired did not turn out well. But having gotten this far with Morris, the officer was now ready to put his own name on the line. He took out his calling card, as before, and handed it to the manager. "If there is any problem, I want you to call me," said the officer.

The job advocacy proved successful. Not only did Morris sustain his new job, which for him was a completely new experience, but in short time he was named "Employee of the Month." He also kept going to the restorative justice circle meetings, sharing his story for the benefit of others who attended. In reflecting on this entire case, Janine observed how the community around Morris experienced a profound shift that amounts to a form of forgiveness. No longer was the community closing its doors but it instead was finding ways to open up opportunities. Morris's former anger and despair was also transformed into a positive state of being able to give back to the community with a rewarding attitude. And all of this was made possible through a form of dialogue that encouraged people to be open and honest, to simply speak from the heart.

A Community Circle Changes Everyone's Hearts

Another circle meeting from this same neighborhood program involved a major breakthrough for former gang members. One interesting statistic among homicide inmates in prison, according to Janine, is that 75 percent of these offenders knew the person who was shot or killed. One can imagine, then, that as gang members return to their urban districts, it would not be surprising for members of rival gangs to face each other in reintegration programs. And without successful programs, former enemies can easily continue as future enemies.

One offender in the circle recognized someone he shot at in earlier years. At one point when the talking piece came to him, he looked at the former rival across the circle, explained the circumstances of the shooting, and then he apologized directly for trying to kill him. When the talking piece reached the other ex-offender, he apologized for his part, and spoke openly about wanting to see changes. When the circle time was over, the two of them approached each other in the middle of the circle and hugged each other. The circle keeper recalled that no one ever used the language of forgiveness during the discussion, and yet what everyone had witnessed was clearly a moment of forgiveness. And after most people had left the premises, the keeper observed that the two men, outside the building, continued to have conversation.

While these sorts of meetings were never designed to be straight victim-offender dialogues, the depth of conversation nearly always matched the levels of resolution and healing that typify good victim-offender meetings. Rarely did victims and offenders from the same case take part in the same circle, but it was common to mix victims and offenders of similar cases in a circle. Again, all of them had an experience of violence done to them that they could share, and this openness was the secret to creating a conversational space that was healing and reparative for everyone in the circle. When one person shows strength and courage in sharing a moment of loss and weakness, it makes it all the more inviting for others to find the courage to share their own story. This sharing becomes like a positive contagion or chain reaction that sets good things in motion for all involved.

The added benefit within the community circle model is that everyone in the circle comes away changed. These participants—police officers, probation officers, local store owners, mothers of children who were killed, and more—all share openly as equals in the meeting. This has a profound effect on the offenders who are present. It sends them the message that "you are one of us, and you have a place in our community." In a sense, these participants not only represent the whole surrounding community, but they spread the goodness they experienced back outward to the community.

It is not surprising that the two former gang members in the story above both continued to attend the weekly circle for some time, even after they fulfilled their quota of required sessions. They simply wanted to help multiply the forgiveness that they themselves had experienced. Here we see how justice is best understood as the positive result of a process, and not simply the intended process done "to" or "against" an offender. In this community circle model we encounter a justice that overflows and makes things better for the whole community.

CHAPTER 17

An Offender Takes Part in His Victim's Family

"Like it or not, on the day of the accident, you became a part of our family," said Agnes to the man who was responsible for making her partner a wheelchair-bound paraplegic for the rest of his life. Through a trust-building process that involved a restorative circle conversation, the offender, Mac, learned about the needs of the victimized family. And within months, amazingly, Mac did become a part of the family. On a weekly basis he was helping with the transportation of Agnes's partner, Shaun, to his physical therapy sessions and other destinations. It is one thing to be part of a family through a tragic narrative, but quite another to be part of a family through ongoing connections that bring healing and goodness for all involved.

In May 2008, Shaun and his four-year-old son, who are part of the Oglala Lakota Nation on the Pine Ridge Reservation, were driving home in Rapid City, South Dakota, only to have their lives turned upside down. Driving an unusually high speed in a residential zone near a school, Mac's car hit Shaun's car head on. While Mac survived without major injury, Shaun lost the use of all of his limbs. His son, in the back seat, was spared any physical injuries.

Earlier that day, Mac had inhaled the fumes of a computer dust spray can, and later, while driving, he had no memory of side-swiping three vehicles and running headlong into Shaun's car. When he finally came to his senses in a jail cell, he learned firsthand about what he did. Being the kind of person Mac was, he was filled with shame and remorse. His occupation was in human services, and he was used to a professional lifestyle in the workplace. He did, however, have a drug use problem.

PART 5—Forgiveness for Communities

After the trial and nearly three years of prison time, Mac initiated a request through his probation officer to have some sort of dialogue with the victim party. The local Center for Restorative Justice in Rapid City was contacted. For obvious reasons, the agency director, Joann, and the assigned facilitators were very leery about taking on this case. This was a high profile story in the news media, and everyone in the city, it seemed, knew how much loss and pain was caused for Shaun and his family. What did it mean for the offender to initiate a restorative process? What were his motives?

But as the initial intake process unfolded, and the victims were contacted to see if they wanted to consider a restorative process without having to make any commitments to follow through, they "agreed in a heartbeat," according to Joann. Both Shaun and Agnes were not ones to stay stuck in the negative emotions of despair or anger or vengefulness. Anything that could help them move forward in life was welcomed by them. After about four months of preparation meetings, the stage was set for a group to come together, including family members and support people.

One thing that became known to the facilitators during this preparation time was how Shaun's son was affected. At eight years of age, four years following the crash, he still struggled with fear, and also struggled with challenges at school. Simple things, like sleeping well at night, had clearly been impacted by the incident. Another ripple effect from the crash was the rising anger within Shaun's brother Shane. In a second intake meeting that included Shaun and Agnes, it was evident that Shane had strong retaliatory feelings. Again, the facilitators wondered how they would deal with this kind of intensity when bringing all the parties together for dialogue. In fact, Shaun and Shane's parents were initially afraid to join the process, knowing firsthand the high-pitched energy level of Shane's vengeful emotions.

By Christmastime it seemed as though people were ready to meet; everyone had a natural nervousness to come together, but to wait any longer would create additional anxieties. Along with the primary folk involved, parents and siblings showed up, and three facilitators were present. Agnes and Shaun also wanted their son to be present. A talking piece was used to create a mood of reverent listening. Due to his condition, Shaun struggled with being able to communicate, as his speech was often hard to discern. But he had said that he wanted to speak for himself.

After the preliminaries of the circle time, Shaun was the first to speak. He then put a question straight to Mac: "Why did you do this to me?" Mac, in a sincere, apologetic voice, explained his irrational thinking and

An Offender Takes Part in His Victim's Family

behavior that led up to the crash. Both Mac and Shaun went back and forth in this segment of dialogue, and the others provided the space they needed to talk directly to each other. Then Agnes shared with Mac how much "you changed our lives." She talked about how at the time of the accident, Shaun was about to graduate from the School of Mines and Technology in Rapid City. The plan was that he would then find new employment that would bring in new income for the family. She then described their new, unchosen life that revolved around Shaun's constant physical care. It was plain how much hurt and brokenness had defined their existence. Again, Mac was very apologetic and responsive.

Throughout this first half of the circle process, the young son said nothing and only cried. People knew that he had carried a lot of pain over the four years, and it was difficult to now face all of the realities of the situation. When the facilitators chose to call for a break time, Mac went straight over to the son, knelt down to the boy's eye level, and said that he was sorry for what he did. That is when the boy first began to talk. He said, "Now I know you are not a monster." It was a touching moment of breakthrough for him and Mac. By that time, most of the family knew that the son had struggled with the fear of "the driver" coming again, monster-like, to hurt him. The crippling energy of that fear ended that day. He also had his persistent questions answered and put to rest, such as, "Dad, when are you going to walk again?"

After the break, others in the circle had opportunities to share from their own experiences. Shane spoke about his feelings, and how he was glad that he had come that day to the meeting. Due to all he was witnessing between his brother, Agnes, and Mac, it left no place for any feelings of retaliation to be pressed upward like a geyser. The pressure had dissipated. Parents on both sides were thankful for being present, as they too carried much pain and grief within themselves from caring about their children. In particular, Shane's father thanked Shane for attending the meeting.

Once the facilitators knew that all had been said to bring deeper healing and resolution through the dialogue, they shifted to discussion toward the future. Again, Agnes, Shaun, and Mac were the primary participants in figuring out what Mac could do to bring reparation for his actions. That is the point when Agnes said, "through this offense you became a part of our family." As the greatest family needs had to do with transporting Shaun to his medical and therapy appointments, Mac soon agreed to assist as a driver. Some agreements were drafted for a follow-up plan, and even Mac's

PART 5—Forgiveness for Communities

parents offered to help out when requested. Altogether, the circle process lasted for four hours.

Most restitution agreements of this nature typically have a time frame attached so that both offender and victim parties know when all has been made right, and the offender can move on with a clean slate. But in this case, no time frame was considered. It simply went without saying that because Shaun's handicap needs are lifelong, he needs lifelong help. With an open heart, Mac has taken on this role of transporting Shaun, and he continues to do it to this day, often a couple times in one week. This now includes rides for the son to school functions, and taking Shaun to a breakfast outing now and then. In a heartwarming way, Mac has become a part of the family through supportive interaction on a weekly basis.

When asked if the language of forgiveness had ever entered into the circle process, Joann said that nobody asked for forgiveness or extended forgiveness, "but the forgiveness was there even though it was never spoken." There is little doubt that the goodwill on the part of both the offender and the victims laid a foundation for the harms of the past to be transformed into reparations for the present and future. As this case was so well known throughout the community, and as the participants were well known in school and social service networks, this narrative of forgiveness quickly spread throughout the city in a contagious way.

One expression of this communal support for Shawn and his family took place on the third anniversary of the accident. Though Shaun was not formerly able to graduate from the local School of Mines and Technology, that opportunity was finally granted to him after he had made sufficient headway in his rehabilitation. Since the time of the joint dialogue meeting, Mac even assisted with driving Shaun to school-related appointments to ensure his graduation. On the day of the graduation, the auditorium was filled, and Mac was present with the family. Without the use of a wheelchair, Shaun managed to walk across the stage to receive his diploma. There was not a dry eye in the auditorium. One can only imagine the collective energy of support that overruled the sad, negative energy that had formerly been unleashed.

CHAPTER 18

Closing Thoughts

Bearing Witness to Strength and Resilience

ONE THING IS VERY clear to anyone reading all of these stories of forgiveness and resolution. Everyone in these restorative dialogues exhibited the qualities of amazing strength and resilience. This is especially true for those who were hurt the most from violent crimes or conflicts caused by others. Most people who have never experienced such levels of personal impact or deep anger can only imagine a fraction of what it is like to climb the mountain of negative emotions and reach the summit of forgiveness and release. Facilitators and mediators in the field of restorative justice always consider it an honor to bear witness to these courageous efforts on the part of victims, offenders, and parties in conflict. One of the main reasons for writing this book was to allow you, the reader, to have a front-row seat in witnessing the amazing strength shown by wounded people who seek healing through dialogue.

This opportunity to have a close view of how people transcend their hurts and pain is really a way to honor them. It goes without saying that they become our best teachers. The stories about Pam and Ann and Jack and Susan and Alex and all the rest are stories where people, already feeling vulnerable from the impacts of past harms, chose to move into a process that involves additional vulnerability. But what we learn from these "teachers" is that their willing and voluntary choice to endure more vulnerability becomes a pathway to greater results and to a better future. Forgiveness becomes the safer and healthier route compared to remaining within one's own inner emotional turmoil. These people had great courage to venture into the unknown, having no guarantee of how things would turn out, but trusting deep down that it was worth trying for their own well-being. In their journeys of finding strength to move forward, we all have so much to learn from them. With that in mind, a second reason for this book is to simply honor those folks who chose, sometimes against all common sense, to experience deep resolution through restorative dialogue.

If facilitators and onlookers did not have their own stories, in varying degrees, of being hurt or of hurting others, they probably would not sense the profundity of what they observe in others who go through a restorative process. In fact, all of us have our own stories of being hurt and hurting others, most often with people in our families, workplaces, and community groups. It is no surprise that we find our stories resonating at some level with the intense stories represented in this book.

A third reason for writing these stories of forgiveness, therefore, was to inspire readers to consider how they can journey into the same realms of resolution and forgiveness for situations that remain unresolved. Certainly if murder cases can see the kind of transformation described in this book, any case in our lives can be engaged for potential resolution and forgiveness. The first appendix to this book is specifically designed to give anyone the tools to respond to hard relational hurts whether or not a third-party, neutral person is guiding a process.

But does forgiveness have to be named to be experienced? Clearly not. A fourth reason for writing this book was to demonstrate that genuine forgiveness can and does happen even when the word *forgive* is never used between people. Most of the stories in this book, in fact, were selected to make this very point. What seems to come up over and over again as these stories are compared is that the main participants experienced a profound shift away from negative emotional energy to more positive emotional energy. This is not to say that everything is completely over and all is "rosy." It is to say, rather, that those who have been burdened by the hurts of the past have experienced some sort of unburdening, and they are able to move more freely into their futures. However forgiveness is understood, it consistently bears this feature of moving forward in a healthy way.

In mapping the contours of forgiveness in these stories, it appears there are more common denominators than distinct features. To be sure, forgiveness may never be defined the same way by people who journey through the experience of being hurt or troubled by others. And some, like Bridget, will honestly and openly say, "No, I cannot forgive him." We have also looked at

Closing Thoughts

group circle processes where there were no single offenses to be addressed, but instead webs of tension and mistrust kept co-workers or students in the grip of past conflicts. In those cases, participants rarely used the language of forgiveness, and yet they all experienced a breakthrough that helped them move forward. And so, not only are there forgiveness scenarios where "forgiveness" is not named, but also where there is no obvious person to potentially offer forgiveness. In the variety of all the stories in this book, however, all persons interviewed attest to the fact that they experienced perhaps the equivalent of forgiveness on a personal level. And so we are left with quite a paradox: true forgiveness seems to happen in most situations where alienated people experience a new and deeper connection, even in situations where one person does not "forgive" another person for a wrong done.

How are we to understand this paradoxical dimension of forgiveness? Is this simply a matter of semantics? What is happening at a bedrock level is that people are experiencing "release" and "relief." They have carried the toxic emotions resulting from the chemical reactions of a deep hurt or conflict, and at some point, a negative energy zone shifts into a positive energy zone, and things are better for all involved. Forgiveness as "release" and "relief," then, may be the simplest way to tie together all of the narratives about restorative dialogues with positive outcomes. While the participants of these dialogues may have sought out release and relief, whether consciously or subconsciously, they were consistently surprised at the level of relief that came in their respective stories.

The point to be made is that there is no set formula for this relief to come about. It comes out of many different kinds of situations and out of many different combinations of circumstances. Like anything profound in human experience, elements of mystery will always remain. Nevertheless there are some lessons that can be learned from situations where restorative processes have served as a centerpiece. The following list, therefore, reflects the broadest understanding of forgiveness as used in this book.

Lesson One: Forgiveness Is a Self–Defined Process on the Part of the One Forgiving

Forgiveness is always freely chosen and if extended toward another, always freely given. For this reason, mediators and facilitators never initiate invitations for forgiveness, nor set the stage with any expectations for forgiveness to be named or experienced. If a discussion of forgiveness does arise between a client and a facilitator, the facilitator does not try to define what forgiveness is. His or her focus is on creating safe, constructive spaces for people to have healing through support and dialogue opportunities. As seen well in Pam's story (chapter 6), she was encouraged to define her own needs and if forgiveness arose in conversation, she was encouraged to define the terms in ways that best made sense to her. In this way there is never any social pressure or expectation for an aggrieved party to do something or experience something internally.

Lesson Two: Forgiveness Primarily Involves the Internal Journey of the Forgiver

While forgiveness is profoundly a relational dynamic and can involve direct encounters and conversation between parties, it is primarily occurring within the thoughts and heart of the person who carries the hurt and is seeking a way to go forward. In this light, forgiveness is therefore not dependent on an offending party's presence or response, nor is it dependent on a specific moment in time. Some of the cases in this book involved offenders who at first were not forthcoming with remorse or openness. But the victim party still journeyed forward, knowing deep down that, as Anne put it, "I've gotta do this for myself."

Lesson Three: Forgiveness Can Be Enriched for Both Parties When There Is Good Preparation

Whenever mediators or facilitators are involved in helping people through restorative processes, preparation is essential to help maximize what can come out of a joint dialogue. This does not mean that everything is under complete control. In the burglary case of the Smiths and Steve, a large amount of negative energy dominated the first part of the meeting. But because each party had enough trust banked up with the facilitator, it served to hold things together so that everyone could reach a much more satisfying outcome. For cases involving serious and violent crimes, preparation helps the victim to be more empowered as they approach a joint dialogue, while helping the offender to be more open and response-able.

Lesson Four: Forgiveness Can be Enriched for Both Parties When Dialogue Involves Two–Way Empathy

As was said in the school circle meeting that addressed racism, "If I hear your story, I can now feel you and relate to where you're coming from. That's where forgiveness is possible." Perhaps the most important element of joint dialogue that leads up to the summit of release and the downhill path of relief is when new understanding creates a new bond between people who otherwise feel no points of connection other than the history of pain and hurt. This point of connection, at best, is compassion, literally, "a feeling with" the other person with new appreciation. It is a time when the humanity of the other person shines through and transcends any prior image of that person.

Are these lessons only applicable within the context of restorative dialogue that is guided by trained facilitators? By no means. Self-defining, internal journeying, preparing, and experiencing mutual empathy are all elements that anyone can embrace as they seek a way forward. What is most clear from all of the stories described is that something deep down within a person motivates them to take the risk and seek the good of their own lives as well as the life of the one who caused the harm. This inner drive will always have a mysterious aspect to it. But it truly points to the highest capacity of the human spirit to show compassion on all levels. Once we recognize our solidarity with all others who have suffered, no matter what the level of suffering is, we open ourselves up to practices that help us further our journeys toward wholeness. We see how deep listening and authentic presence, mindfulness and centeredness are practices that lead us through our greatest hurts.

The amazing thing in our day is that as these stories are told more and more, research is showing how the initiation and experience of forgiveness is actually good for our health and well-being. It is good for the soul, good for the heart, and good for the mind. At the same time, forgiveness allows people to touch a spiritual depth where personal growth and relational interaction meet. If we think of the presence of negative toxic energy like pollutants in our water systems, we can then think of forgiveness as a clean-up process, similar to a swamp with healthy plants that can filter and transform those pollutants so we can have safe, drinkable water. At a profound level, forgiveness along a spectrum described in this book seems indispensable for healthy living at all levels of social life. Do we want our social systems to be more sustainable? Fostering opportunities for forgiveness might prove to be a key factor.

More studies will be added to the already growing body of literature on forgiveness studies, and this is to be welcomed. But ultimately we, as members of real communities, will need to go beneath all of the theories and rational understandings of forgiveness. To truly understand the inner workings of forgiveness experienced by other people requires that we will have to go deeper within ourselves to face our own histories of wounding and being wounded. With similar courage to that exhibited by the victim survivors in this book, we too will need to humble ourselves, tame our controlling egos, and open ourselves to new pathways of understanding and healing. This journey in effect becomes a spiritual journey to connect with the suffering of all people, and in that solidarity, we may find ourselves rising up with a renewed energy, the energy of life that helps us to become fully human.

APPENDIX 1

The Language of Energy for Conflict and Resolution:

More than a Metaphor

by Ted Lewis

IN MANY RESPECTS, UNDERSTANDING how the energy of conflict and conflict resolution works is similar to understanding how the force of gravity works. Scientists even today humbly admit that they really don't know how to explain gravity, even though they can fully study its effects. How can something as invisible as gravity have such a profound influence on all matter? Or in the realm of electromagnetics, how can a distant, invisible force make a tiny needle in a compass jiggle? And so we may also ask, how can something as invisible as the energy of forgiveness be so significant in the lives of people who journey forward out of deep conflict and trauma? In what sense is that energy "real"?

One way to approach this topic is to consider how the emotional energies surrounding conflict and resolution processes have numerous parallels in the study of physical energies that operate in our world and in human technologies. By considering the common language used by scientists of nature's processes and facilitators of peacemaking processes, I hope to show that the energy dynamics of interpersonal and community conflicts are far more than a metaphor. It may turn out, in fact, that the very reason energy language is so appropriate for facilitators is because the emotional forces at work, be they positive or negative, are real forces, like light and gravity,

APPENDIX 1

which move in and around our bodies. And indeed, move in and around our hearts, and extend outwardly toward other people.

Ever since Einstein formulated his equation about the relation between energy and matter, the study of energy has grown by leaps and bounds. Two new frontiers of study include research on how black holes work at the center of galaxies (including our own Milky Way), and on how our hearts and brains pass bioelectric communications to each other, resulting in the modulation or emission of strong emotions. Common to both of these areas is the concept of energy fields. Consider how black holes are voracious eaters of all incoming sources of mass and energy, and yet more recent research has found that black holes also spill out energy beyond the boundary of their gravitational pull. Now consider how an individual's intense emotions can suck in the emotional energies of other people, while also spilling outward with damaging consequences. Little wonder that a self-help book came out, blending the terminology of different disciplines: *Black Holes and Energy Pirates: How to Recognize Them and Release Them*.[1] What we are increasingly seeing in multiple areas of study is the cross-fertilization of the language of energy.

As a mediator and facilitator of both restorative justice and dispute resolution cases, I have comfortably used the language of energy in my descriptions of conflict and resolution processes. But this has been a very loose, informal usage that has not moved much beyond phrases like, "The energy between the parties was really tense," or "By the end of the meeting you could feel how the energy in the room was relaxing." Over the years, I have spoken of the "energy shift" when a mediation goes from tense "uphill" dialogue work to relaxed "downhill" dialogue work. What I hope to accomplish in this essay is to push us further to consider how the presence of energy in relational conflicts is far more than a metaphor; it is a very real interplay of unseen forces that can be studied, mapped, and even harnessed in the service of providing better resolution services to people in conflict. As this is an exploratory exercise, I will leave it to others to add both better research and better theory to what for me is simply a first-time expedition into new territory.

Of special interest to me is how a source of energy can be converted into other forms of energy. Just rubbing our hands together on a cold winter day involves the transfer of kinetic (moving) energy into heat energy. This friction, a concept easily transferable to the realm of relational conflict,

---

1. Reeder, *Black Holes and Energy Pirates*.

becomes a source of energy intensification. Such an intensification happens very fast when we strike a match on a striker pad. In fact, the word *conflict* stems from the Latin word meaning "to strike together." Recall times when you may have rubbed your shoes on a shag carpet, building up a charge of electricity that could arc out from your finger and shock another person. This provides a simple analogy for how conflicts, due to the way clashing interests rub "against" each other, create a new storage of negative energies that seek an avenue of release.

Once energy is released it can go in a couple of directions. It can be converted into useful energy or it can become wasted or unused energy. A more complex system of energy flow and energy conversions starts with our sun. The sun, a constant generator of nuclear energy, throws off excess radiant energy toward our planet. Our climates and ecosystems are sensitively tied to the amounts of sun-energy received, and all plants photosynthesize this energy to grow. In turn, animals digest plant life, and through a conversion process that stores up energy in calorie units, this potential energy is released through muscle-driven movement and work. At the most fundamental level, be it for food or warmth, energy keeps us alive.

But more significantly, as stated in the Wikipedia article, "Energy is necessary for things to change."[2]

This reminds me of a maxim that I often use in my trainings called the Five C's: "Conflict Creates a Chance for Constructive Change." (Crime could also be substituted for Conflict.) I know for myself that the main thing that keeps me committed to the field of conflict resolution is the transformative opportunity that I see from time to time in the lives of clients who went through a dialogue process. Without the prospect of personal and relational change, there is not much motivation to help people who are stuck in conflict. Consider now another grade-school-1level example of energy conversion (or energy transformation): the hydroelectric plant. Storable water above a dam turns into gravitational energy when it falls, which converts into the mechanical energy of spinning turbines, which converts into electrical energy that is moderated through transformers. Note the concepts of

1. potential energy that is stored up;
2. kinetic energy that is released through activity; and
3. useable energy that is controllable for desired outcomes.

2. http://en.wikipedia.org/wiki/Energy.

APPENDIX 1

A fourth category of wasted energy (usually in the form of heat) could also be added to this list, but for the purposes of this essay, I'll put that one on the back burner. When considering the dynamic elements of a mediation or facilitation process, not much is lost in using a hydroelectric plant as a metaphor. Conflicts and harms build up within a deep reservoir of blocked energies for both parties. The initiation of a resolution process commonly stirs up a flurry of intensified emotions and doubts, and participants often put up points of resistance. After a good dialogue (a circular exchange of listening and speaking between polarities), a transformative outcome leads to useful energies, including new solutions to help people move forward in life. In effect, the negative energies coming into the process have been converted into the positive energies coming out of the process.

We have now considered several examples from the physical sciences involving energy fields and energy transformations, noting the resonance of "energy language" in the field of conflict studies. But is this only a metaphoric usage for those of us in the peacemaking fields? I believe the reason why this language is becoming increasingly central to descriptions of how conflict and resolution processes work is because there is far more going on than meets the eye. Someday, social-scientific research will reveal a clearer picture of what is going on, just as today's researchers in physics cannot explain the dynamics of gravity, but will likely advance their theories in decades to come. Meanwhile, just as the forces of gravity are researchable according to their effects, so the forces of emotional and relational energies are to be reckoned with so that facilitators can best operate in the realm of conflict resolution. This perspective, however, needs to be balanced with the fact that several ancient health traditions, including qigong in China and aikido in Japan, have been operating for centuries with a complex understanding of how to cultivate life-force (*chi*) energies revolving in and around the human body. This wisdom alone could advance the practice of mediation to new heights.

In a 2003 article, "The Energy of Conflict: An Emerging Paradigm," coauthors Deborah Isenhour and Marilyn Shannon explored how moods throughout a mediation can have a heavy or light feel to them.[3] They called this unseen phenomenon "the energy of conflict."[4]

That was ten years ago, and at that time, medical research was making inroads into bioelectromagnetics. For instance, are there negative health

3. Isenhour and Shannon, *Meditating in 3-D*, 1.
4. Ibid.

effects for people living next to high-voltage power lines? Other medical studies explored how a healer's bioenergies could actually flow outward for healing purposes, giving rise to a variety of alternative therapies that are active today. With applications in the realm of mediated dialogue, the authors suggested that both negative energies from what parties bring and positive energies from what mediators bring (and elicit from parties) can have a profound effect on processes and outcomes. One contribution from this framework was "The Energy Audit," designed to map out stuck energies and imbalances within or between disputants.

I have often heard mediators talk about emotional energies in terms of being blocked or released. And any mediator or facilitator who has done multiple cases has experienced that magic pivot point during a meeting when the mood shifts from tension and mistrust to relief and greater trust. Sometimes you can even identify a statement that activated this transfer of emotional energy. It may have been a sincere apology by one party, or perhaps an empathetic acknowledgement of what the other party has experienced. As I have witnessed these shifting points over the years, I can say that I have felt, literally, the profundity of these moments in my heart. There is a stirring, and then there is a relaxing. It is as if the human heart was a source of energy activity; the hub of where negative or positive energies were both stored and released. Little wonder, then, that moments of expressed apology or forgiveness between people, those heightened moments of energy transference, are spoken of as coming "from the heart."

One of the interesting aspects in these deeply powerful moments of sharing and listening is the way they involve vulnerability, but also courage. To verbally express apology or forgiveness involves vulnerability on several levels. First, there is the vulnerability of looking into yourself and recognizing that within you is some degree of incompleteness. For those who have been on the giving end of hurting others, it is the incompleteness that comes with shame and self-disappointment. For those who have been on the receiving end of being hurt, there is the incompleteness of being wounded and needing validation. A second level of vulnerability comes from not knowing how another person will respond. Will they accept my words? Due to this vulnerability, it takes great courage to verbally say something that can truly help transform the negative energy of the heart into a positive energy that is good for both giver and receiver. An apt analogy involving energy conversion is composting in the garden. Decaying food

APPENDIX 1

scraps and organic matter eventually change, through heat, into usable and pleasant-smelling soil. I call this process "death unto life."

When we speak of people having a "heart-to-heart" conversation, in effect we are saying that their conversation is going to have enough depth for blocked energies (weighing down the heart) to be released (resulting in lightheartedness). In more common terms it means that people will be as honest as they can to lay things out on the table and find a way to move on. This process, whether aided by a mediator or not, invariably involves some degree of "death unto life." A good dialogue will have a series of miniature deaths so that new life can rise up. As speaking from the heart demands a level of humility, there is a very real expenditure that takes place. A part of a person's control has been expended, given up. But this, in energy terms, is what helps to activate an energy conversion, changing the stored negative energy into a useful positive energy. As in a chemical catalyst, the old is burned and the new is born. A candle provides a good image where wax and flame and oxygen combust to create new forms of useful energy: warmth and light. We all know that the release of negative energies can be a powerful thing, resulting in either helpful or harmful outcomes (a controlled fire for cooking or a forest fire that gets out of hand). The job of a good facilitator is to facilitate (in French it means "to make easy") the transformation of negative energies into positive life-giving forces. Given the volatile nature of emotional energies, it is clear that a third-party guide is essential for holding a controlled, constructive space for resolution.

Energy Shifts from the Heart

These shifts in energy that transform negative emotional energy into positive emotional energy have been illustrated well by Dr. Mark Umbreit in his recent book, *Dancing with the Energy of Conflict and Trauma*.[5] By choosing the word *dancing,* Umbreit is telling us that there are no hard-and-fast formulas for how we handle the energy dynamics in a conflict. It really amounts to a deep listening with one's heart and inner being, as well as listening to the deeper levels of others. A relevant image is the tai chi master in martial arts who loosely and playfully moves *with* the movements of an opponent rather than *against* those movements. This seems to fit well with the idea of energy transference. Mediators and facilitators learn to take the loaded statements that get released in conversation and through reframing

5. Umbreit, *Dancing With the Energy of Conflict and Trauma*.

and redirection, assist in a conversion of those energies into something useful for ongoing resolution.

Umbreit's book offers twenty stories of how negative energy shifted into positive outcomes that rebuilt broken relationships. In one case involving family members, he writes,

> Highly toxic and hurtful energy had been transformed into authentic communication. . . .The energy of the entire event had shifted in a very palpable way.[6]

Again, the impulse to be present to a hurtful situation was not a result of a left-brain "how-can-I-fix-this" mentality. Umbreit emphasizes how the intuitive, nonlogical side of our brains provides the best resource we have for fostering energy shifts in hard relational situations. Altogether, this is an excellent book for showing the relationship between negative storehouses of energy that create conflict, and positive sources of energy that resolve and even transform conflict.

Umbreit's emphasis on "listening to the heart"[7] corresponds well with recent neurocardiological research that reveals how the human heart and brain send quick messages back and forth to each other. Functioning not as a mere pump, the heart is found to house brain-like features that regulate emotions, and thus is constantly colluding with brain activity. The authors of "The Energy of Conflict," cited earlier, wrote a sequel article to advance their explorations of emotional energies.[8] They cited an Institute of HeartMath study suggesting that when people attune better to their hearts, the "synchronization between our hearts and brains increases,"[9] and this maximizes both intuitive and intellectual capacities. Conversely, stress studies are showing that decision and problem-solving functions are hampered when heart patterns are not steady and relaxed. Mediators have always understood that if emotional energy between parties is not relaxed, it is nearly impossible to lead people into a constructive zone of creating mutual agreements. Even when we, ourselves, are involved in a difficult family or workplace conflict, our capacities will rise or fall depending on our ability to manage our emotions.

---

6. Ibid., 25.
7. Ibid.
8. Isenhour and Shannon, "The Energy of Conflict."
9. "Science of the Heart."

APPENDIX 1

But there is more. As the heart generates the largest electromagnetic field compared to any other organ in the body, so-called "heart energy" not only affects the brain, but can affect another person's emotional energy up to several feet away.[10] In the same way the heart can activate a shift from the lower brain (the fight-or-flight-response zone) to the higher brain (the cognitive zone where moral virtues and empathetic connections are mobilized), it appears that one person's heart energy can also spread beyond the body to activate positive or negative shifts within another person. Isenhour and Shannon apply this within the setting of relational conflicts.

> When we are able to listen to and respond from our heart energy, we can begin to communicate in ways necessary for the transformation of relationships. Igniting the heart energy allows new understanding to become available. Opening up to our heart energy helps to soften and balance our emotional states bringing clarity and releasing discord. There must be a partnership between the heart and the head for harmony to exist. The energy that is being used to hold onto a conflict can now be free to fuel healing.[11]

I could expand on how all this works itself out in dialogue processes, but for now, I invite you to review the language of the quote itself. "Igniting the heart energy" and "free to fuel healing" are two notable phrases. Heat energy terminology almost always conveys the conversion of one energy form to another. And it is not only a matter of a new outcome, the end product of a resolution process. The energy transformation creates a new condition *during* the dialogue encounter that significantly allows for a better outcome. The softening, the balancing, the bringing of clarity and harmony, which includes cognitive understanding, all are elements that happen during the shift-stage itself to ensure maximal transformation. This softening image is well illustrated by the image of a solid object slowly dissolving in a liquid state. In fact, the very words *solution* and *resolution* are tied up with this process, stemming from a Latin word that means "loosening, unfastening, dispersing." Facilitators, at best, are aiding this profound and often subtle transition from hardened states to softened states to ensure positive outcomes. How well this all blends with the centuries-old language of the hardened heart (resistant to change) and the softened heart (open to change).

10. Ibid.
11. Isenhour and Shannon, "The Energy of Conflict."

John Paul Lederach, at the outset of his *Little Book on Conflict Transformation*, describes the creative tension between the terms *conflict resolution* and *conflict transformation*.[12] After a trip to Central America in the 1980s, he recognized that conflict resolution did not go deep enough to address underlying social structures and relationship patterns. Employing the language of energy, he wrote,

> Conflict transformation begins with a central goal: to build constructive change out of the energy created by conflict.... The key here is to move conflict away from destructive processes and toward constructive ones.[13]

The transformative shift I have referenced above is very evident in this framing. But what Lederach helpfully adds to our discussion is the depth of underlying conflict sources that need to be addressed. No scientist doing experiments in the laboratory is exempt from experiencing some mishaps. Likewise, mediators can face explosive situations when working with deep-seated, multilayered conflicts. To extend the analogy, peacemakers need to have patience, persistence, and of course, patterns of safe preparation if they are to effectively remain in their roles to deter destructive processes and foster constructive ones.

By way of summary, what follows is an outline that shows the cyclical flow of energy within a conflict resolution context. Visualize these three areas in a circle where the end of the third area can feed into the first area.

1. Stored Energy (Potential)
    a. Can be blocked (uncommunicated)
    b. Can be released (communicated)

2. Released Energy (Kinetic)
    a. Can be uncontrolled (destructive)
    b. Can be controlled (transformative)

3. Transformed Energy (Useful)
    a. Can be used (for healing, empowerment)
    b. Can be stored up (for future use)

12. Lederach, *The Little Book of Conflict Transformation*, 14.
13. Ibid.

APPENDIX 1

The resolution of a difficult hate crime that I facilitated can be an example to review this energy flow diagram. A neo-Nazi youth was involved in an act of vandalism against a synagogue. Years later, opportunity arose for both offender and victim parties, voluntarily, to journey through a series of resolution meetings over twenty months. Significantly, the youth was proactively moving out of his hate-based subculture. The stored energy from both parties was very deep, given the emotional intensity of hate-group dynamics and the residual emotional weight of Jewish persecution history, notably the Holocaust. Carefully timed processes of communication had to be orchestrated in order for appropriate amounts of this stored energy to be released, first in preparation meetings and then in joint dialogue meetings. And not all of the stored energy was by any means negative or blocked. Both parties deeply wanted goodness to come out of a restorative process.

Throughout the many months of meetings, I was mindful of how my own stored and released energies were vital to instill extra doses of calmness and trust into the equation of bridge building. There was a rubbing-off effect that involved an exchange of distrustful energies for trustful energies. The activation energy of an apology and the loosening of forgiveness language were part of the first joint dialogue, and these helped to convert some of the earlier blocked energies into useful energies for future reconciliation work. At times I noted how the release of lesser controlled energies created very challenging disturbances, a type of temporary chaos. For example, a federal investigator met with the whole group once and this unleashed an explosive set of emotional energies that threatened to terminate the process, even after months of successful reconciliation work. Hard as it was, I took this unharnessed energy as a potential source that could be converted into a new platform for continuing the process. A restrengthening of the group happened, allowing a newly transformed energy to be used by all involved. In successive stages, the older forms of energy were being changed into new, life-giving forms, and both parties eventually expressed relief about the relative closure and healing that came about.

I have intentionally packed this brief narrative with energy language so that you can see the connections between a resolution process and any other energy conversion process. At the same time, because I had firsthand engagement with these "energy flows," I can say that they were very real even though I could not demonstrate or replicate them in a laboratory. Someday there may be Star Trek-type monitors that can track the presence, type, and intensity of emotional energies that operate during conflict resolution situations. Please know, however, that when I say these energies are "more than metaphor," I do not mean to say that they cease being metaphoric. Language and narrative are the best vehicles we have to describe our human experiences, especially when things invisible to our eyes are at play. We would do ourselves a great disfavor to drop the richness of language. And maybe we cannot drop the language of energy, because it is so inextricably tied to the human heart in all respects (physiologically, psychologically, and spiritually). If this is the case, as I have been advocating throughout this essay, then the language of heart energy can only become more common.

My sense is that energy analogies in this field, along with heart language, fit so well precisely because such unseen forces are operative beyond our comprehension. Fortunately, there is no conflict between the scientific exploration of these dynamics with our rational thinking and the experiential exploration of unseen energies with our intuitive senses. Even when the common person says, "I have low energy today," or "I'm feeling heavy-hearted," we can know they are hinting at a greater dynamic than they could ever imagine. Our goal as mediators and peacemakers is to tap into this greater dynamic, literally with both head and heart, in order to strengthen our language and thus strengthen our practice.

APPENDIX 2

Fostering the Energy of Forgiveness Within Ourselves and Others:

Practices to Foster the Energy of Forgiveness

by Mark Umbreit

IN SHARING THE JOURNEY of those who have directly faced severe conflicts or traumatic events, or as we experience those events in our own lives, there are many practices that can foster the energy of forgiveness. In bearing witness to the many stories that we have shared in the previous chapters, our lives can be enriched. These people who have endured severe conflict, or who have been hurt so deeply, can be among our most powerful teachers, providing us with life wisdom as we journey the path of forgiveness and healing, to give us strength to be there for others and to be there for ourselves.

By fostering the energy of forgiveness, these practices can nurture our soul, our body, and our whole being. No one approach or practice will necessarily be effective for all people. Some of the practices that we are sharing with you can certainly relate to most people; they come from many different cultural settings and have been practiced throughout the ages.

Practices to Foster the Energy of Forgiveness

Meditation

The practice of meditation, or other contemplative forms of quieting the mind—being still—is powerful. It runs against the very fabric, the very energy, of our warp-speed modern culture. And yet, there is clear evidence showing that regular practice of meditation, in whatever form you find fits best with your culture and your life-context, can yield almost immediate physiological and emotional benefits. Meditation is a way of learning to work with breath, to be comfortable in silence, to engage in a practice that tames and slows down our minds. It allows us to access the energy of our heart as well as the wisdom of the mind.

There are many different forms of mediation, and some of those that practice and teach it can be as rigid and dogmatic as any conventional teacher or clergy person. What we encourage, at least as a starting point, is a relatively generic form of meditation that we can all access and adapt to our life-context and culture. What we've shared with you previously about mindfulness is the starting point to developing a meditation practice. Going deeper requires a teacher, oftentimes a group, with whom to practice for reinforcement. But eventually it can be done alone, if you don't have a group with which to practice.

Even taking just five minutes a day for mindfulness, for centering yourself, can become a powerful practice in setting a different tone as you begin the day, so that you don't begin the day with the busy and frantic energy that many of us immediately give in to. By taking this time, we can begin the day in a more focused and reflective mode.

Centering and meditation are ways of reclaiming our power, of reconnecting with our wholeness. Many people feel they have little time for meditation, that it is a distraction, of little use, even a waste of time. Many others have come to a very different point, realizing it's not a matter of either the contemplative life of one who meditates or the busy life of one who is overextended in personal and work life. They have come to the point of realizing it's not an either/or proposition. It's both. The Dali Lama, Gandhi, Martin Luther King, Dorothy Day, Mother Teresa, and many others are glowing examples of people who integrated some form of contemplative practice into their lives. They tapped into the spiritual energy that is part of all of us, with powerful and effective social action to better the world, and directly addressing widespread injustices and suffering. Fostering the energy of forgiveness within ourselves is also about integrating some form

APPENDIX 2

of contemplative practice with direct engagement of the challenges facing us in life.

People who have practiced daily meditation for many years have typically found that they are far more effective, efficient, less stressed, and happier if they begin the day with a meditation practice. When you begin meditation, whatever form you're trained in, it's not as if you're going to be in instant bliss. Not at all. Your mind will always wander, because it's full of all these thoughts. Meditation is building on what you can learn from the practice of centering. It's a way of acknowledging those many thoughts, but not fighting them, letting them go, and focusing back on your breath, or focusing on a beautiful place in nature, or focusing on a mantra or some sacred words or a verse from your culture or faith tradition, depending on your life-context.

Meditation is not rocket science. It doesn't require a formal degree. It's a relatively simple process to learn. All it takes is sitting in a comfortable position, sitting straight with the back erect, closing the eyes, and breathing slow and deep. When beginning, it can be helpful to breathe in slowly and deeply into the belly to the count of eight or ten and then exhaling slowly to the count of eight or ten. You may choose to include a focus on a sacred word or a visualization of a beautiful place in nature that always brings you peace. Learning to use the mantra or the beautiful place in nature as a way of redirecting the energy of the mind, to let go of all of those thoughts, allows that incredible stream of consciousness to pulse through our mind. The goal is to be aware of those thoughts and simply let them pass by, not holding on to any one.

We offer this as an oversimplification of meditation, but it is a way of describing the core essence of meditation. Different practices, from different cultural and spiritual traditions, will have a range of techniques and practices. But the core essence of meditation is a way of slowing down the mind, slowing down the ego. It's shifting from the frantic energy of multitasking to a different state of consciousness where one is living more in the present moment, with a heightened sense of awareness.

In meditation, even if there are loud noises in a neighborhood, one can still tune in to the birds chirping or other sounds of nature. And finally, meditation does not require being at some retreat, on comfortable cushions and beautiful music in the background. Of course, that's nice if you can be in a quiet setting, and it's a good way of getting recharged, but meditation can occur even in a noisy place.

Practices to Foster the Energy of Forgiveness

Working with the Energy of the Body

Working with the energy of the body is an important tool in taking care of ourselves. There are many forms of meditation in motion that can be very helpful, depending on what works for you. For some it can be as conventional as getting into dance, as dance taps into a different energy in us, a very creative energy that takes us away from our thoughts and our minds and our troubles. For others it would be the practice of yoga or tai chi or chi gong or other forms that integrate the contemplative practice of the mind with working with the energy of the body in a beautiful way that brings us into the present moment. For others in can be as conventional as jogging or taking long walks.

Learning to work with the energy of our bodies can deeply nurture not only our physical bodies but our spiritual, mental, and emotional bodies, as well. Our bodies are largely overlooked in our modern society. We alter them for personal appearances, obviously, but we don't treat them well. We don't give them regular exercise; we don't use the gift of our bodies in the way they're meant to be used. So developing a practice of each day, walking a couple miles or jogging around a lake, or doing whatever works for you, is very important. Whether it's meditation (where it brings the mind to peace and nourishes the soul at a deeper spiritual level) or meditation in motion (such as yoga, tai chi, chi gong, or even certain types of dancing), the key issue is regular daily practice.

You may need to learn certain techniques of yoga or tai chi or dancing before beginning your practice, but these are very learnable. And then again, the central issue is practice, practice, practice. Unless we weave them into the rhythm of our lives, unless they become part of the daily flow of our energy, as normal as brushing our teeth or washing our hands, these practices will have very little effect. It might give us a temporary boost, a good feeling, but then we get sucked into the vortex of the busy energy of multitasking that takes us out of the present moment. We reflect on the past, what we did or didn't do. And we're likely projecting on the future, pursuing specific plans and goals.

For all of the practices that we will share with you, it's important to realize that their power is not in the periodic practice of the technique. Again, the power is in the daily practice.

APPENDIX 2

Massage

There are many forms of massage that can be incredibly helpful in terms of nurturing our souls and our bodies as we're dealing with the energy of conflict and trauma within ourselves or among other people. Physical massage on a regular basis, perhaps once a month or even more frequently, can be very helpful in relieving tensions within our body. There's also energetic massage through Reiki and Healing Touch, which is a type of massage that involves very gentle touch or even above-body work. It can have a powerful effect on our body, mind, and spirit. Energy massage helps release stuck toxic energy and often leads to a very comfortable, peaceful, altered state. There's also a Chinese form of massage called *tui na*, which is a more rigorous, deep massage that has some unique characteristics and can be very helpful. There's a Hawaiian type of massage called lomilomi, and there are many other types of massage as well.

The point is that no one type of massage is a one-size-fits-all. All massage techniques help release energetic emotions that get stuck and carried in our muscles and our body. They help release those tensions so that we feel better.

Guided Imagery

Guided imagery involves the use of relaxation and mental visualization to improve mood and physical well-being. In its most simple form, guided imagery is the use of one's imagination to promote mental and physical health. It can be self-directed, by creating one's own images, or directed by others. There are many different CDs that you can get to lead you through this. It will usually involve a person with a very gentle voice initially guiding you through progressive muscle relaxation. You could be lying on the floor, in bed, in a comfortable recliner, or on a couch, spread out with your arms at your sides, eyes closed. And the voice will guide you to relax each muscle from the tips of your toes to the top of your head. It will then guide you to go to a deeper place. A place where you feel safe. A place that is well known to you in which you feel comfort and joy. It's not a prescriptive kind of guidance in most cases. It's trying to guide you into finding a place within your own life experience, your memories. A place where you feel acceptance and comfort. It brings back good energy of the past. And then you

Practices to Foster the Energy of Forgiveness

will be guided through different ways of dealing with emotional or physical wounds you are carrying.

A series of CDs that many have found particularly helpful, which was developed by one of the pioneers in the field of guided imagery, is by Dr. Martin Rossman. Particularly for those with exceptionally busy schedules, with little time to engage some of the above self-care practices, guided imagery is a very practical bridge from one's current busy lifestyle to deeper forms of meditation or yoga practice. For many, guided imagery is much easier to integrate into their life. You simply put a CD into your player and then listen to the guide as you are relaxing. Ultimately, guided imagery is a particularly helpful tool in slowing down and relaxing, in fostering the energy of forgiveness in the many conflicts we will inevitably be faced with.

All of these practices may not fit within your own life-context and preference. Yet some can definitely be integrated into your life, and your efforts to foster the energy of forgiveness through relaxing, slowing down, taming the ego, and becoming increasingly mindful, and humbled, by the fact that in all conflict, with rare exceptions, all parties involved are contributing to the conflict and the inability to let go. It may not always be the spoken word. The nonverbal energy of our presence, our voice tone, and body language frequently communicate the true message.

Nearly all communities or regions have resources and trainings on these and other tools. Mindfulness-based stress reduction workshops and classes are offered throughout North America and many other countries. These workshops are particularly good in introducing people to the practice of meditation, yoga, and self-care. As you search for training and resources to find tools for the journey in your community, let Google do the work. Simply put in words like: self-care, meditation, massage, yoga, tai chi, guided imagery, and mindfulness-based stress reduction.

Enjoy the journey. Remember, the power of these practices is not in the technical learning of the process in a one-time workshop, retreat, or book. The power to access the wisdom, compassion, and peace within all of us is in the practice, practice, and more practice, until it becomes a normal part of our daily routine.

APPENDIX 3

Mindfulness, Deep Listening, and Stories:

The Spiritual Core of Peacemaking

by Mark Umbreit

THE JOURNEY OF PEACEMAKING and spirituality is about honoring the enormous healing power of story; listening deeply to the woundedness within others and ourselves; acknowledging the pain of others without judgment, assessment, advice, or problem solving; and nurturing the innate strength, wisdom, and yearning for peace that is within each of us. The journey is about being ever mindful of the power of unintentional negative consequences if we cannot tame our egos and their endless thirst for recognition and control; learning to tame our minds and their endless thoughts and chatter so that we can be fully present with each other through the turbulence of inter- and intrapersonal conflict.

Creating a safe, if not sacred, place where people in painful conflict can tell their stories, without interruptions, has been at the core of healing throughout the ages. Arguments and positions keep us in the head, while telling stories touches our hearts. When I work with victims of severe criminal or political violence seeking mediation and dialogue, much of my "intervention" involves deep compassionate listening and acknowledgement of the stories of trauma for all involved, without judgment or prescription.

Cultivating Mindfulness

The journey of peacemaking and spirituality is about being present with conflict in our wholeness, in our body, mind, and spirit. It is about "being with" rather than "doing for" the conflict, allowing our own and other's woundedness to teach us profound lessons of life in community. Learning to be fully present in our life and work, with no illusions of control, is not easy in Western culture. Yet there are a number of practices that cultivate such presence. By far the most relevant spiritual practice that we can integrate into our peacemaking and conflict resolution work is mindfulness. Cultivating mindfulness means that we consciously strive to stay present in the moment.

There are many other practices that can help us to integrate spirituality into our life work including yoga, tai chi, chi gong, and others—all of which can be accessed quite easily through local course offerings, books, videos, and CDs. Each approach represents a meditative practice in movement. Each works with our wholeness: body, mind, and spirit. Each cultivates the power of breath to promote healing and a compassionate presence with those in our presence. After living in China and learning chi gong from Taoist masters, my approach to conflict has profoundly changed. No longer do I focus exclusively on the cognitive and verbal expression of conflict. Instead, I work with the energy of conflict, my own and others. The powerful nonverbal language of our bodies and spirits are far more potent in both understanding conflict and allowing the path toward healing to be engaged.

The simple act of centering can also be easily integrated into our practice. While centering is part of all the practices already mentioned, it can be used by itself in a quick and practical way by taking a few moments to close the eyes, focus on deeper breathing, imagine a beautiful place in nature or a person who immediately brings you joy, and allow interruptive thoughts within the mind to simply float away by refocusing on the breath.

Telling the Story

The journey of peacemaking and spirituality can often be seen in numerous incredible examples of stories told by people working in the field of restorative justice dialogue, particularly in cases involving those directly affected by the commission of severe criminal or political violence in North America and abroad. The following case example involves Sarah, a young

APPENDIX 3

mother whose father was brutally murdered more than twenty-two years ago, and Jeff, the man imprisoned for his murder. When Jeff was eligible for parole, Sarah and her family became consumed with intense feelings of vulnerability, anger, and uncertainty. They decided to speak at this hearing, and the offender was not approved for release. Sarah contacted me shortly after the parole hearing and expressed her strong inner sense of needing to meet the man who killed her father so many years ago.

From the beginning it was clear that Sarah was yearning to find peace within herself and her immediate family. Jeff, the offender, felt tremendous remorse for what he had done and was willing, though scared, to meet with Sarah. Extensive in-person preparation of the parties over many months occurred before my co-mediator and I brought them together in a face-to-face dialogue at the prison. After extensive pre-dialogue preparation through deep listening and gentle guidance, the primary role of the co-mediators was that of bearing witness to the strength, capacity, and compassion of these wounded individuals as they helped each other heal. In more than five hours of the mediated dialogue, the two mediators spoke less than twelve minutes combined, yet we both were totally emotionally present, and available to hold the sacred space that emerged.

My co-mediator and I practiced mindfulness through centering and breath work both during the preparation and in the dialogue so that we were able to keep our egos and voices out of the way of the dialogue and allow Sarah and Jeff's strength and wisdom to emerge and flow as it needed to. After very brief opening comments by the mediators, we entered an extended period of silence as Sarah sobbed and tried to find her voice to tell her story. As mediators, we did not intervene to move the process along. Instead, we remained silent until she was able to speak. After nearly four minutes, Sarah found her voice and her story of trauma, loss, and yearning for healing flowed out with strength and clarity. Jeff then offered his story of what happened, how it had affected his life, and the enormous shame he felt. They continued to share deeper layers of their stories, interspersed with lingering questions from both. Sarah and Jeff told us later that the energy of our presence, the nonverbal language of our spirit, was vital to the process being safe and respectful of their needs and abilities.

After five hours and shortly before the session ended, Sarah looked directly at Jeff and told him she forgave him for killing her father. She made it clear that this forgiveness was about freeing herself from the pain she had carried with her for more than twenty years. She hoped this forgiveness might help him as well, but Sarah said she could not set her spirit free without forgiving him. Sarah had never indicated in our many months of preparation that forgiveness was an issue she was struggling with, nor did we raise the issue. When she and her husband came to the prison for the dialogue with Jeff, she had no plan whatsoever to offer forgiveness. Yet in the powerful moment of confronting her greatest fear, Sarah spoke of how she felt within her soul that "this is the moment to free myself."

In post-dialogue interviews with Sarah and Jeff, they both indicated the enormous effect this encounter had on their lives. Sarah spoke of how meeting Jeff was like going through a fire that burned away her pain and allowed the seeds of healing to take root in her life. She spoke of how before meeting Jeff, she carried the pain of her father's death like an ever-present large backpack. Now after meeting Jeff, the pain is more like a small fanny pack, still present but very manageable and in no way claiming her life energy and spirit, as before. Jeff reported a sense of release and cleansing, as if his spirit was set free as well.

Path of the Peacemaker

The journey of peacemaking and spirituality is grounded in practitioners first learning to walk the path themselves, within their personal and professional lives. Finding the still point of power within us is essential, oftentimes through meditation, prayer, meditative movement, or other forms of spiritual practice. This power has nothing to do with control over others. Instead, this power allows us to tame the energy of our minds and egos so that we can be fully present, with the most healing capacity for the people with whom we are working.

Power flows from the recognition that it is not about our wisdom or technical expertise, but rather the need to honor the enormous capacity of highly conflicted, and often traumatized, people to find their strength and help each other heal through deep compassionate listening, from speaking and listening from the heart. It is in the energy of our communication, particularly through the nonverbal language of our spirit, that we can offer a sacred place for bearing witness to the healing power of story. The language of our spirit communicates many things: our authenticity; the congruence between our thoughts, feelings, actions, and the higher values we adhere to; our intention; and openness and nonjudgmental nature.

APPENDIX 3

The path of peacemaking and spirituality requires a human connection, grounded in empathy, support, and impartiality, with the conflicted people with whom we are working. It requires the ability to make no assumptions about the needs of others, so that we as facilitators do not impose our judgments or spiritual needs and practices upon others. Peacemaking with others and within ourselves is about embracing the spiritual wisdom that bridges can in fact be built, no matter how intense the conflict or trauma might be. This is a journey that is ultimately grounded in a spirit of humility and compassion rather than technical expertise and credentials. May we all find the strength to walk this path.

Bibliography

Armstrong, Karen. *Twelve Steps to a Compassionate Life*. New York: Anchor, 2010.
Arrien, Angeles. *Living in Gratitude: A Journey that Will Change Your Life*. Louisville, CO: Sounds True, 2011.
Baldwin, Christina. *Calling the Circle: The First and Future Culture*. New York: Bantam Doubleday Dell, 1998.
Baldwin, C., and Ann Linnea. *The Circle Way: A Leader in Every Chair*. San Francisco: Berrett-Koehler, 2010.
Boyes-Watson, Carolyn. *Peacemaking Circles and Urban Youth: Bringing Justice Home*. St. Paul: Living Justice, 2008.
Boyes-Watson, C., and Kay Pranis. *Circle Forward: Building a Restorative School Community*. St. Paul: Living Justice, 2014.
Crum, Thomas. *The Magic of Conflict: Turning a Life of Work into a Life of Art*. New York: Touchstone, 1998.
———. *Three Deep Breaths: Finding Power and Purpose in a Stressed-Out World*. San Francisco: Berrett-Koehler, 2006.
Frankl, Victor. *Man's Search for Meaning*. Boston: Beacon, 1946.
Gold, Lois. "Influencing Unconscious Influences: The Healing Dimension of Mediation." *Mediation Quarterly* 11 (1993) 55–56.
Isenhour, D., and Marilyn Shannon. "The Energy of Conflict: An Emerging Paradigm." http://www.mediate.com/articles/isenhourD1.cfm.
———. *Mediating in 3-D: The Energy of Conflict: A New Balance of Power*. Cary, NC: North Carolina Bar Association Foundation, 2004.
Johnson, R. A., and Jerry M. Ruhl. *Contentment: A Way to True Happiness*. New York: HarperCollins, 2000.
Kabat-Zinn, Jon. *Coming To Our Senses: Healing Ourselves and the World through Mindfulness*. New York: Hyperion, 2005.
———. *Wherever You Go, There You Are: Mindfulness Meditation in Everyday Life*. New York: Hyperion, 2005.
Lederach, John Paul. *The Little Book of Conflict Transformation*. Intercourse, PA: Good Books, 2003.
Luskin, Fred. *Forgive for Good: A Proven Prescription for Health and Happiness*. San Francisco: HarperCollins, 2002.
Muller, Wayne. *How Then, Shall We Live?: Four Simple Questions that Reveal the Beauty and Meaning of Our Lives*. New York: Bantam, 1997.
———. *A Life of Being, Having, and Doing Enough*. New York: Harmony, 2010.

Bibliography

Nepo, Mark. *Gift of Awakening: Having the Life You Want by Being Present in the Life You Have*. Boston: Conari, 2000.

Pranis, Kay. *The Little Book of Circle Process*. Intercourse, PA: Good Books, 2005.

Pranis, K., Mark Wedge, and Barry Stuart. *Peacemaking Circles: From Crime to Community*. St. Paul: Living Justice, 2003.

Reeder, Jesse. *Black Holes and Energy Pirates: How to Recognize Them and Release Them*. Freedom, CA: Crossing, 2001.

Remen, Rachel Naomi. "Spirit: Resource for Healing." *Noetic Sciences Review* Autumn (1988) 4–9.

Riestenberg, Nancy. *Circles in the Square: Building Community and Repairing Harm in School*. St. Paul: Living Justice, 2012.

Satir, Virginia. "The Therapist Story." *Journal of Psychotherapy and the Family* 3 (1987) 17–25.

Schaef, Anne Wilson. *Native Wisdom for White Minds: Daily Reflections Inspired by the Native Peoples of the World*. Scoresby, Victoria, Australia: Random House Australia, 1995.

"Science of The Heart: Exploring the Role of the Heart in Human Performance/Head-Heart Interactions." http://www.heartmath.org/research/science-of-the-heart/head-heart-interactions.html.

Shimony, Abner. "Bell's Theorem." *Stanford Encyclopedia of Philosophy* Winter (2013). http://plato.stanford.edu/archives/win2013/entries/bell-theorem/.

Skog, Susan. *Peace in Our Lifetime: Insights from the World's Peacemakers*. Fort Collins, CO: Cliffrose, 2004.

Stutzman Amstutz, L., and Judy H. Mullet. *The Little Book of Restorative Discipline for Schools: Teaching Responsibility; Creating Caring Climates*. Intercourse, PA: Good Books, 2005.

Taylor, Daniel. *The Healing Power of Stories*. New York: Doubleday, 1996.

Umbreit, Mark. *Dancing with the Energy of Conflict and Trauma: Letting Go—Finding Peace*. N.p.: CreateSpace, 2013.

Umbreit, M., and Marilyn Peterson Armour. *Restorative Justice Dialogue: An Essential Guide for Research and Practice*. New York: Springer, 2010.

Van Ness, D. W., and Karen Heetderks Strong. *Restoring Justice: An Introduction to Restorative Justice*. New Providence, NJ: Matthew Bender & Company, 2014.

Wheatley, Margaret J. *Turning to One Another: Simple Conversations to Restore Hope to the Future*. San Francisco: Berrett-Koehler, 2009.

Zehr, Howard. *Changing Lenses: A New Focus for Crime and Justice*. Scottsdale, PA: Herald, 1990.

———. *The Little Book of Restorative Justice*. Intercourse, PA: Good Books, 2002.

Zimmerman, J., and Virginia Coyle. *The Way of Council*. Las Vegas, NV: Bramble, 2009.